A Special Letter from

Stefani, one of the greatest pleasures I've had in life is being blessed to be your mother. From the day I learned I was pregnant with you, I knew you would be special. I know I was extra protective and stern with raising you; but you are my firstborn, and I wanted to make sure I was raising you right. Kids do not come with instructions, and my rearing skills came from my parents. That's all I knew about raising a child. I was so afraid if I died and weren't around to take care of you, there would be no one to love you like me. Although it was not easy raising you as a single parent, I would do it the same all over again. Had it not been for God's grace and mercy, and of course the love and support of our family, I couldn't have raised you alone. It still takes a village!

As a toddler, everybody loved you—even strangers. You would walk up to a stranger, grab their hand, and smile. Your smile would put a smile on their face. You are a light, and you have been spreading the gospel since you were a child. During the summers after Bible school, you would evangelize to your sister and the neighborhood children in the backyard, sitting on crates. You have brought so much joy and sunshine to my life. I am convinced that you were sent to me by God to help save my life.

I focused on raising you to be self-sufficient by emphasizing the importance of education. I remember telling you to keep your eye on the prize. Not only did you keep your eye on the prize, you learned to keep your eyes on the Lord. You are being rewarded abundantly.

You have become a beautiful, compassionate woman of God. I am so very proud of you and grateful to have been the vessel God chose for your arrival to the world.

Keep on spreading the Good News, and God will continue to bless you!

Love, Mama

BREAKING FREE
FROM THE FEAR OF

Poverty

*How to Change Your Mindset
and Live the Abundant Life*

STEFANI ALEXANDER

Breaking Free from the Fear of Poverty:
How to Change Your Mindset and Live the Abundant Life
by Stefani Alexander

Cover design, editing, book layout, and publishing services by KishKnows, Inc., Richton Park, Illinois, 708-252-DOIT

admin@kishknows.com, www.kishknows.com

ISBN: 978-0-578-70392-3
LCCN: 2020920396

Some Scripture references may be paraphrased versions or illustrative references of the author. Unless otherwise specified, all other references are from the King James Version of The Holy Bible.

Scripture references marked NIV are taken from THE HOLY BIBLE, NEW INTERNATIONAL VERSION®, NIV® Copyright © 1973, 1978, 1984, 2011 by Biblica, Inc.® Used by permission. All rights reserved worldwide.

Scripture quotations are taken from the Holy Bible, New Living Translation, copyright © 1996, 2004, 2015 by Tyndale House Foundation. Used by permission of Tyndale House Publishers, Inc., Carol Stream, Illinois 60188. All rights reserved.

Printed in the United States of America

TABLE OF CONTENTS

A Special Letter from My Mama i

Introduction ix

CHAPTER 1: Poverty by Default 1

CHAPTER 2: Wounded by the Womb: A Mother's Love 9

CHAPTER 3: The Footwork of Poverty 19

CHAPTER 4: Emotional Poverty: Traumatic Emotions 27

CHAPTER 5: Relationship Poverty 37

CHAPTER 6: Abandoned by the Father: Child Support 53

CHAPTER 7: The Family Tie That Binds 61

CHAPTER 8: Codependent Relationships 73

CHAPTER 9: Returning to the Source 79

CHAPTER 10: Financial Realignment: When the Layoff Pays Off 87

CHAPTER 11: Plan B 103

CHAPTER 12: Finally Free: The Set*back* was a Set*up* 111

CHAPTER 13: Destined for Greatness: Steps to Living
the Abundant Life 119

Praise for "Breaking Free from the Fear of Poverty" 133

About the Author 137

Resources 139

Contact the Author 139

I would like to give honor to my Heavenly Father, Jesus Christ. I also dedicate this book to my natural and spiritual family, my friends, and to the late Reverend George Harris. RIP!

INTRODUCTION

In 2018, the Lord began to deal strongly with me about the spirit of poverty. Many people assume that poverty only pertains to money…but it's actually a *mindset* and a *mentality*.

Have you ever wondered how rich people think? Or how poor people think? And what the difference is in their individual thinking patterns? Imagine going to the grocery store to pick up some chicken wings, and you see two packages. The first package you pick up says $6.52, and the second package says $6.48. Which one will you choose? People with a poverty mindset will automatically choose the one that costs $6.48. Why? Because they feel as though they are paying less and are getting the "best bang for their buck." But they may actually be paying more per pound of meat.

The reality is that there are many factors to consider when determining whether or not you are getting the best deal. I have subconsciously done this numerous times at a store, even when I had more than enough money to get what I wanted, regardless of the price. By default, most of us tend to go for the lower priced items, and I believe that this has a direct correlation to every decision we make in our personal lives.

I have become intrigued at how we choose the best options for every area of our lives based on a "default system" known as "poverty." This book is my story of how God delivered me from a poverty mentality. He has delivered me from the spirit of poverty which has, at one point or another, governed all areas of my life.

This book has been a long time coming! I prayed, and I asked the Lord what I should write about and tell His people. I started writing this story after a very traumatic event that happened in my life.

I was laid off from my job four times in seven years. Four times! The last time was due to a car accident that left me with the inability to use my left hand. I sustained a severely broken left wrist that resulted in two major surgeries, extensive occupational therapy three times a week, and the inability to use my hand for approximately seven months.

On May 14, 2019, I was sitting in the orthopedic surgeon's office, discussing with my godmother how I was believing that God was going to do something supernatural where my finances were concerned. I further explained that FEAR was driving me to get out of debt. I had been laid off so many times, and unemployment barely paid for all of the bills that I had. I decided that I never wanted to be in that position again, so I aggressively began to demolish debt.

One of the nurses heard me talking. He turned his head and said, *"I don't mean to be in your business, but **you need to write that book**, because I think about being broke every day."* His response blew me away! His face was filled with fear, anguish, and distress. He looked like he was hopeless and needed solutions to his problem. After he left the room, I knew that I had an encounter with the Lord, and that His response was prophetic. There was a fierce fire that ignited within me to *get it done*—because people are trapped in the shackles of life, and they are waiting for someone to set them free! The devil thought he would stop me from writing this book…but he thought wrong!

QUESTIONS FOR REFLECTION

- *Do you feel (or have you felt in the past) that your life is "governed" by the spirit of poverty?*

- *Has fear ever driven you to do something? What was it, and what was the end result?*

CHAPTER 1

POVERTY BY DEFAULT

In order to understand my victories in overcoming poverty, you must understand how it all started.

NEVER ENOUGH

I grew up in a single parent home with my mother and sister. At the age of ten, my mother taught me how to write out a check and balance a checkbook, using her real-time paycheck. I realized much later that I was not being taught financial literacy to prepare me for adulthood; but instead, I was taught to show me why my sister and I couldn't have what we wanted outside of the essentials.

One particular incident that stayed with me was when my mother said, *"We only have $100 to get us through the next two weeks, not including the cost of food and gas."* As a child, this was an eye-opening experience for me. It was good that I learned how to manage money when I didn't have a lot, but on the other hand, I felt that all of my hopes of *ever having anything* were shot! I thought to myself, *"Wow. We can never get anything because we don't have enough."*

Although I was shocked, it helped me to understand why we couldn't have certain things at the store and that taking care of the essentials was our top priority. But I learned early on that I was "limited," and "it would always be that way." I didn't realize this at the time, but as an adult, my cousins and I would talk about how we didn't know we were poor. Although we had hand-me-down clothes, we had new shoes and uniforms for school. We did fun activities like bowling and going to Great America, and we had gifts for Christmas.

I believe that the devil used this moment as an entry point to teach me his ruling powers of poverty. We had everything we needed, *and* we did not want for anything else. We were comfortable with the bare minimum. This way of thinking cascaded into a whirlwind journey of living a mediocre life that included jobs, relationships, etc. The enemy had plans to keep me tightly bound and rooted in poverty as a child, which would eventually show its ugly head in every area of my life as an adult.

POVERTY: WHAT IS IT?

What exactly is poverty? Where did it come from? According to Merriam-Webster, poverty is *"the state of one who lacks usual or socially acceptable amount of money or material possessions."* And according to Dictionary.com, poverty is *"the state or condition of having little or no money, goods or means of support, condition of being poor. Deficiency of necessary or desirable ingredients, qualities. Scantiness; insufficiency."* Synonyms for poverty include *debt, distress, emptiness, inadequacy, deficit,* and *lack.* I'm sure that we can all relate to both the definition and the synonyms for poverty.

When I first thought about how I was going to explain the poverty mindset, I thought about slavery. Slaves were required to do everything for their masters, with no "say so" in the matter. They were made to hate and fight each other, even to the point of death, because of the color of their skin. They were given the leftovers and scraps of food and received the bare necessities for everyday living.

The snares of poverty have been deeply rooted into the human psyche, so much so that when the slaves were "supposedly" freed, they couldn't fathom even the *thought* of being free. Being set free was a foreign language where "lack" was normalized as the "this is as good as it gets" way of living. Many of us today still live with a slave mentality in the way that we speak, the way that we think, and how we receive from others.

THE SPIRIT OF POVERTY

The slavery mentality is actually governed by the SPIRIT OF POVERTY! If the enemy can keep us in darkness, then we'll never see the light. This means that we will never see our way out. We will never see the solution to the problem, and we will never have the courage to step out of our comfort zones and live an abundant life. The slaves were surrounded by darkness; and while some saw the light, others couldn't. Why was this the case? Because of FEAR! The devil presents us with fear which paralyzes us while draining all of the life (the light) out of us. The mentality of the slaves was rooted in fear, which kept them in poverty. This whole idea of the poverty mentality did not start with slavery. It actually goes all the way back to the beginning of time, before Jesus Christ came on the scene as a man. **Genesis Chapter 3** paints a story of how poverty entered into the hearts of man and led to the fall of mankind.

> **Genesis 3:1-8:** *"Now the serpent was more subtle than any beast of the field which the Lord God had made. And he said unto the woman, 'Yea, hath God said, Ye shall not eat of every tree of the garden?' And the woman said unto the serpent, 'We may eat of the fruit of the trees of the garden: But of the fruit of the tree which is in the midst of the garden, God hath said, "Ye shall not eat of it, neither shall ye touch it, lest ye die."' And the serpent said unto the woman, 'Ye shall not surely die: For God doth know that in the day ye eat thereof, then your eyes shall be opened, and ye shall be as gods, knowing good and evil.' And when the woman saw that the tree was good for food, and that it was pleasant to the eyes, and a tree to be desired to make one wise, she took of the fruit thereof, and did eat, and gave also unto her husband with her; and he did eat. And the eyes of them both were opened, and they knew that they were naked; and they sewed fig leaves together and made themselves aprons.*

And they heard the voice of the Lord *God walking in the garden in the cool of the day: and Adam and his wife hid themselves from the presence of the* Lord *God amongst the trees of the garden."*

The serpent (the devil, our enemy) put a thought in Eve's mind which made her want more. He had a simple conversation with her that convinced her that she was indeed missing out on something. He led her to believe that she **needed** to know about the knowledge of good and evil. As a result, she influenced her husband, Adam, by giving him the forbidden fruit…and then all hell broke loose. Prior to this, God had already given Adam dominion over all of the earth, but He gave *very specific instructions* about the Tree of the Knowledge of Good and Evil.

Genesis 2:16-17: *"And the* Lord *God commanded the man, saying, 'Of every tree of the garden thou mayest freely eat: but of the tree of the knowledge of good and evil, thou shalt not eat of it: for in the day that thou eatest thereof thou shalt surely die.'"*

Before Eve was created for Adam, God put the responsibility on man and gave Adam and Eve everything that they needed to live. They did not lack anything, and they did not have a desire to explore things that were never presented to them. If we look at **Genesis 3: 6-10**, we see that once they ate from the tree, they *realized* that they were naked; and as a result, they hid themselves from the presence of God. They were exposed, naked, and ashamed. This was not something that they were supposed to experience.

ROOTED IN FEAR

Adam and Eve had the pleasure of walking with the Lord freely, with no shame, no guilt, and no condemnation—just pure bliss and unconditional love. If you read further in **Genesis 2** and **3**, you will see how the beautiful story of creation unravels into the tragedy which led to the fall of man, which was SIN! Sin is separation from God and changes our spiritual DNA to an unfulfilled and mediocre life. The ways in which poverty reveals itself can be very appealing and desirable…until the truth is revealed. It is a sin to be in poverty, because this was never God's original plan for our lives.

I used the conversation with the serpent as an illustration to show how the wrong mindset can change your behavior and lead to a life full of fear, shame, guilt, and hopelessness. As you can see from this story, poverty is fed by and rooted in fear.

Eve had the fear of the unknown but only because it was *presented* to her. *Fear is only exposed when it is presented to us as an option by the enemy.*

> I believe that Eve was afraid that God was holding something back and that maybe there was more to life than what she knew.

Prior to this situation, poverty and fear were foreign to Adam and Eve. The sad part about this story is that Eve had the nerve to bring her husband into it and the consequences of disobeying the Lord would forever plague generations to come. Now, I don't know about you, but if I had everything I needed and I didn't know that I needed anything else, I'm not sure the serpent would have been able to persuade me as easily as it did Eve. But then again, as I think about it, I would have likely made the same decision. Why? Because like Eve, we are human!

We can do nothing in our own strength, not even resist temptation. God has given us free will to make our own decisions, and this is why we need the Holy Ghost.

> All the devil needs is an **open door**. The open door starts with a **conversation**. The conversation sets the stage for the mind, which is the **mindset**. The conversation presented here is not about not having what you need, but about what you **think you don't have**.

It is a perverted way of thinking about God's provision for our lives. The devil is crafty, and we must be careful not to fall into his temptations. All he has to do is make a suggestion; and if he baits us with the desires of our heart, then he can ensnare us and keep us trapped, with no way of escape. But glory be to the Most High God, we have a faithful helper and deliverer! The Lord promised us a way out.

1 Corinthians 10:13: *"There hath no temptation taken you but such as is common to man: but God is faithful, who will not suffer you to be tempted above that ye are able; but will with the temptation also make a way to escape, that ye may be able to bear it."*

We have to be careful to guard our hearts and pay attention to our words, situations, and relationships. The devil has come to steal, kill, and destroy (**John 10:10**) us because we belong to the Lord! And according to **1 Peter 5:8,** we have to *"Be sober, be vigilant; because your adversary the devil, as a roaring lion, walketh about, seeking whom he may devour."*

Remember...*the devil is not on our side.* He doesn't care about us. He is our enemy...and he is *our* enemy because he was an enemy *first* to God. He wants the abundant life that we are promised; and since he cannot have it, he wants to destroy everything that is in fellowship with the Kingdom of God.

THE PITFALLS OF PRIDE

As we seek to understand Adam and Eve's fall into sin, we must know that it all started with the devil in heaven. The devil wants our inheritance, which is the *perfect, ever abundant, and eternal* covenant relationship with the Lord. Satan was the model of perfection and beauty, yet he thought he was greater than God. His pride got him kicked out of heaven. The Books of **Isaiah** and **Ezekiel** give us a clear picture of what happened.

Ezekiel 28:12-15: *"Son of man, take up a lamentation upon the king of Tyrus, and say unto him, thus saith the Lord* GOD*; Thou sealest up the sum, full of wisdom, and perfect in beauty. Thou hast been in Eden the garden of God; every precious stone was thy covering, the sardius, topaz, and the diamond, the beryl, the onyx, and the jasper, the sapphire, the emerald, and the carbuncle, and gold: the workmanship of thy tablets and of thy pipes was prepared in thee in the day that thou wast created. Thou art the anointed cherub that covereth; and I have set thee so: thou wast upon the holy mountain of God; thou hast walked up and down in the midst of the stones of fire. Thou wast perfect in thy ways from the day that thou wast created, till iniquity was found in thee."*

Isaiah 14:12-17: *"How art thou fallen from heaven, O Lucifer, son of the morning! How art thou cut down to the ground, which didst weaken the nations! For thou hast said in thine heart, I will ascend into heaven, I will exalt my throne above the stars of God: I will sit also upon the mount of the congregation, in the sides of the north: I will ascend above the heights of the clouds; I will be like the most High. Yet thou shalt be brought down to hell, to the sides of the pit. They that see thee shall narrowly look upon thee, and consider thee, saying, is this the man that made the earth to tremble, that did shake kingdoms; That made the world as a wilderness, and destroyed the cities thereof; that opened not the house of his prisoners?*

Revelation 12:7-9: *"And there was war in heaven: Michael and his angels fought against the dragon; and the dragon fought and his angels and prevailed not; neither was their place found any more in heaven. And the great dragon was cast out, that old serpent, called the Devil, and Satan, which deceiveth the whole world: he was cast out into the earth, and his angels were cast out with him."*

The devil thought it was a good idea to try to overthrow God's throne. As a result, the devil will be thrown into the lake of fire; with an eternal separation from God, and an eternal life of torment and pain. **Revelation 10:20:** *"And the devil that deceived them was cast into the lake of fire and brimstone, where the beast and the false prophet are, and shall be tormented day and night forever and ever."* The temptation of sin from the serpent caused man to fall from grace, but thank God that He sent His Son, our Lord and Savior Jesus, as a bridge so that we could have full access and relationship with God in His Kingdom.

> Not everything that we want is good for us.

QUESTIONS FOR REFLECTION

- *Was money discussed in your home when you were growing up? Were you included in the discussions?*

- *How did your perception of money during your childhood affect your perception of money as an adult? Do you feel like you were well-prepared to handle your finances, or was (is) it a struggle?*

CHAPTER 2

WOUNDED BY THE WOMB: A MOTHER'S LOVE

Mothers are a gift from God. We don't get to choose our mothers, but God made sure that He put us in the right family, with the right mother. Have you ever thought to yourself, *"What makes a good mother?"* or *"What makes a bad mother?"* Some people may believe that they have the best mother in the world and that she can do no wrong, whereas others may think that their mother is the best; however, she just has a few bolts and screws loose in her head. But the real truth is that our definition of a "good mother" is shaped by our personal experiences, and what we've seen as examples of motherhood.

The Lord created a special role for women in order to fulfill His purpose on earth. The role of a woman became the purpose of man! The Lord said in **Genesis 2:18, 21**: *"And the Lord said, 'It is not good for the man to be alone, I will make him a help meet for him.' And the Lord caused a deep sleep to fall upon Adam and he slept: and took one of his ribs, and closed up the flesh thereof. And the rib, which the Lord God had taken from* *man, made he a woman, and brought her unto the man. And Adam said, 'This is now bone of my bones, and flesh of my flesh: she shall be called woman, because she was taken out of man.'"* God created a suitable partner to help accomplish the goal of having complete dominion over the earth, including our adversary, the devil.

As you already know, it was the role of the man to keep the Garden of Eden intact, but what would be the new role for his helpmeet? Her job was to *grow* the garden, *multiply* it, and make it *prosperous*. The way God planted Adam and Eve in the garden is similar to a woman's womb. Inside a woman's womb is a system of reproductive processes called, appropriately enough, the *reproductive system*. Women are equipped with eggs, waiting for a sperm to fertilize them in order to create a human being. In the same way, God planted man in the garden, the sperm is implanted in the woman.

The woman was placed in the garden to help cultivate it. The womb was created to serve as an incubator that nourishes the newly formed being. When the right timing occurs, the womb releases what has been produced, and the woman gives birth. She becomes the *mother* of the finished product, and births forth life!

PUSH PURPOSE

By now, some of you may be wondering what reproduction has to do with anything? The illustration of the egg and sperm fertilization demonstrates the purpose of a woman. As women, our role is to *push purpose*! We are to cultivate, nourish, teach, lead by example, provide wisdom, and grow others. Mothers help to birth life into something that is not yet developed. Mothers are *life-givers* and *purpose-pushers*. They are the "secret ingredient," packaged with the essential nutrients to our sustainability and prosperity in life. The role of the woman has been mandated and established by God. But what happens when you grow up with a mother who doesn't necessarily exhibit all of the qualities of a godly mother? And what happens when you are not properly nourished? Mothers play an essential role the in the development of our identity—they fill voids in our lives, and their love unlocks the doors to our destiny.

My personal testimony with my relationship to my mother, is one of many "mother wounds" that have been healed by Christ. It is a story of how the spirit of poverty, through a broken spirit, comes face to face with God's redemptive and restorative power of family!

MAMA'S GIRL

I have always been a mama's girl. If I had to describe my mother, it would go something like this: *"My mother is one of my favorite girls. She is sweet, smart, fun, witty, pretty, giving, and **always** on top of her game."* This introduction reflects only a few characteristics of my mother, but this is typically how most of us would describe a person we love, especially our mother. We start with the good things, and leave out the bad or negative things, based on our personal experiences. And, if you have integrity, then you don't want other people to judge them negatively based off of what you believe to be their "not so good qualities" or flaws. Our love runs deeper than what's seen on the surface, but it is not always easy to discern our mother's true identity.

All my life, I've focused on the goodness of my mother because she has instilled so much goodness in me. I learned to become a critical thinker, an organizer, and a leader. I also learned structure, stability, and order. One would think that these are good qualities, but depending on how you are nourished and cultivated, they can also have a negative impact on every aspect of your life.

These qualities negatively impacted my life because I became a perfectionist; I was performance driven and evaluated success through flawlessness. While I am forever grateful for how my mother raised me, I know that she taught me the definition of success in accordance with her own life experiences. *Her* identity shaped *my* identity. *Her* fears shaped *my* fears. Everything I did required the love and attention of my mother. She was my example. But she had so many rules and regulations for what NOT to do that I didn't really learn what TO do.

HALF EQUIPPED

I would say that I was "half equipped" for the world. My life plan for success revolved around the idea that I could not and should not *ever* make a mistake. It taught me that if I had my ducks in a row, then I wouldn't leave an opportunity to make a mistake. I had to be conscious of my decisions and every single move I made at all times. There was never a moment to breathe and to assess how I was truly doing in life. I didn't have an outlet to express my emotions.

There was an incident that happened when I was a child that set up the framework for fear to operate in my life. One day, I went to the refrigerator to pour a glass of milk. I missed the glass, causing the milk to spill over the counter onto the floor, then I dropped the glass and it broke. I looked up, and my mother's face was full of disappointment and anger. I was afraid of what would happen next. I did not get a whooping, but her face told me everything I needed to know. She told me that I had made a mess and needed to clean it up. It was obvious that I had made a mistake, but I didn't understand why she needed to point out what I already knew.

This situation may seem like something simple or irrelevant, but it definitely played a major role in how I saw my mother. It caused more fear and intimidation on the inside of me; and as a result, I became afraid of the fear of failure. I later learned from my sister that this was something she had dealt with too. As we got older, my sister told me about a time when she came to stay over at my apartment, and she dropped a glass on the floor. She looked at me to see if I would be upset with her; but once I assured her that it was just a glass and that we all make mistakes, she was relieved. She thought that I would react in the same manner my mother would, because this is what we saw in our home, growing up!

I believe that my mother could have handled the situation better. She could have been less harsh, more understanding, and more nurturing. She could have said something like, *"It's okay. Just get the mop, clean it up, and be careful next time."* Remember, mothers are designed to be nurturers; and at this point in my life, I didn't feel nurtured. I felt rejected and worthless. I was only about nine years old at the time but think about how this affects the psyche of children in all age groups.

I grew up trying to be the best at everything, proving myself to the world. I did not learn the other side of the story, which was how to handle situations where things don't turn out the way you expected. I wonder what was going through my mother's mind. Did this happen to her when she was a child? Did her parents get upset with her when she made a mistake? Was she so used to high expectations that she could not see her own faults and mistakes? Or maybe, she was frustrated about something else going on in her life. I didn't know what the cause was, but what I do know is that parents have the responsibility to not only correct their children, but to build them back up. How can one learn to be successful at life if they are constantly being scolded and not affirmed?

I would say that I had a very good childhood overall. I know that my mother loved me, and the Lord revealed wisdom to me with two crucial components in my deliverance. I learned that my mother loved me the best way she knew how, and that she wasn't fully aware of the way that I needed to be loved.

Relationships take time to develop, and just because you live with someone, or they are a part of your family, doesn't necessarily mean that you have a good relationship with that person. The devil knows that God made each and every one of us different, with different attributes, perspectives, and how we respond to life's events. He uses our differences against us to further his own agenda. The problem comes when we don't have the appropriate and necessary conversations with one another to help assess *who* we are and *where* we are in our lives.

THE CULTURE CLUB

Communication methods vary among different cultures. In my age bracket (80s to 90s babies), we were taught to "never question adults, do as I say, not as I do, and stay in a child's place." This cultural context that I described is poverty in its rawest form. It displays a level of poverty, and it keeps us bound in our minds and our actions.

I can speak to the above statement because I have experienced all of these spirits as you can see throughout the theme of this book. I did not have a voice growing up; and when I tried to open up and express myself, I was *silenced*. If I tried to express myself about anything, I was told, *"Go to your room."* or *"I don't want to hear it."* These words tormented

> *Anytime you are in a place of authority and you rob another person of their authority and their voice, you open the door to poor self-esteem, lack, inferiority, abandonment, and rejection in their life.*

me and made me feel like no one had time and what I had to say wasn't important. I found myself alone and hopeless yet once again. I learned to keep my mouth shut and not express my opinion or share my thoughts.

This put a damper on my creativity, my talents, and my gifts. I became very reserved and timid, and I was intimidated by the words of others. I was shut up in a box, unable to fully be who God created me to be; hiding my true identity, which was deeply locked away in my soul, my mind, my will, and my emotions. My emotions were so far down and untouched that I actually became emotionless. I was guarded, and I put up a wall that would only allow people to reach a certain point in my heart. I never again wanted to be disappointed or hurt by the people that I loved the most.

The devil sets up a series of events in our lives to make us feel unimportant, inferior, intimidated, and fearful. Fear is a major tactic that he uses to keep us bound in poverty. Fear can present itself as…

- The fear of **failure**.
- The fear of **trusting others**.
- The fear of **being alone**.
- The fear of **not living up to someone else's expectations**.
- The fear of **speaking up and defending ourselves**.
- The fear of **love**.

It hinders our ability to love others unconditionally when they have hurt and harmed us, which can lead to bitterness, anger, rage, resentment, and unforgiveness. It can put us in a place of isolation and confusion. Isolation, because we feel as though no one understands our internal struggles and confusion because we don't know how to open up to people.

Fear and isolation became my best friends. I would keep certain things from my mother, like letting her know my next steps in life: new career and jobs, salaries, dating, and potential boyfriends. This was because I feared her criticism and opinions. There can be moments of complete shutdown because of the lack of trusting someone with your heart. No one wants to open up and pour out their passions and achievement if that person is only going to judge. It is a form of dishonor; it deregulates and pulls down one's attempt to go higher in life. At times, we may think that our opinions are important or helpful to others because we want the best for them. However, what we think is the best for someone may not be the best for them—*it may be the best for us.*

Also, there is a time and place to voice our concerns and opinions, but we must have discernment and should put ourselves in their shoes. Questions that should be asked are:

- Are they ready to hear and receive what I am telling them?

- Is there a lesson that the Lord is teaching them?

- Are my expectations of them a form of what I expect from myself?

- If they don't handle the situation the way that I do, can they still achieve the desired outcome?

- Is this God's will for their life, or am I imposing my own will?

One of the main goals of an effective relationship is to keep a good rapport with the other person which helps to establish a strong and trustworthy relationship. As a result, we can be free to be vulnerable and to receive wisdom while still making our own decisions.

I thank God to this day that I did not build a wall of unforgiveness and resentment toward my mother. I truly believe that God protected my heart and showed me that my mother loved me very much, despite her inability to show love with her emotions. She showed her love by her presence; showing up to my award ceremonies, my step shows, and any other activity that I was involved in. I can honestly say that my mother took very good care of me. The devil had plans to make me bitter towards her, but God's spirit of reconciliation and His powerful redemptive plan prevailed against the gates of hell.

The devil knows that if he can cause disharmony within the family unit, then he can destroy the support and love that we all need to fulfill our God-given purpose in life. The Lord created you and me in His image, and He created us with a uniqueness that no one else has on earth. We are His masterpieces, and He uses the qualities of our mothers to birth forth the gifts and talents needed to bring victims out of poverty and into victory!

In conclusion, we may not always understand the lack of motherhood by our own definitions and standards, but we can be assured that the Lord doesn't make mistakes. I am proud of the woman I have become because of the woman that God called to be my mother. I am very much like my mother; and although we may bump heads a lot, I can honestly say that I would not have it any other way. Through her love, I learned to love unconditionally. The love and the wisdom of God has allowed me to see her as God sees her, and I no longer feel rejected, abandoned, lacking, or have low self-esteem.

The Lord allowed events to occur in our lives that brought us closer as mother and daughter. Our relationship now is better than it has ever been, and I have seen tremendous breakthrough in both of our lives. I encourage you all to assess your relationship with your mother (if it is still possible), and don't allow the orphan spirit to rob you of love. The Lord wants to deal with your mother wounds—the deep cuts where salt has been poured over and over again. Allow Him to change your heart so that you can be open to receive love.

Embrace the process of forgiveness and allow your healing to break forth as you see your life and your mother's life from God's perspective. Extend grace and mercy even when you have been wounded by the womb. It is the place where we are birthed into purpose! Finally, if you desire wholeness, the Lord can do it! He is eagerly waiting to restore your health and heal you of every wound (**Psalm 37:4** and **Jeremiah 30:17**).

QUESTIONS FOR REFLECTION

- *What was your relationship with your mother like as a child? What qualities did she exemplify that you have chosen to emulate in your own life?*

- *Were there parts of your relationship that you did not feel were healthy? What were these, and how have you chosen to "rewrite the story?"*

CHAPTER 3

THE FOOTWORK OF POVERTY

When I was ten years old, the devil had a conversation with me that opened the door to fear, poverty, and all kinds of destructive spirits. These spirits would follow me and disrupt every area of my life.

THE MENTALITY OF "LACK"

The devil had a course set for my life in order to keep me stuck in the mentality of "lack." After becoming accustomed to not having enough, my mindset compelled me to hold on to everything I had. I didn't realize it at the time, but I started holding on to every bit of money I received, whether it was from birthdays, lunch money, or money that my mother won at the casino. I saved more money than any ten-year-old that I knew at the time. I wouldn't touch it for the world. I was afraid to give it up because I was afraid of it not being replenished.

Things got so bad that I wouldn't break a $20 bill at the store, because it would mean that I would have less than I had before. This type of behavior traveled with me throughout my young adult life, and I realized that it was actually a family curse. I remember one of my uncles borrowing money from me as a child. Now you know it's bad when an adult has to borrow money from a child. I did charge him interest and thank God he paid me back on time, but the heart of the matter was why was he living paycheck to paycheck?

As you can see, this way of living was embedded in my DNA. It seemed inevitable that this would be my eternal destination. I was defaulted to struggle in the same way that my family had been struggling.

HOLDING TIGHT AND LETTING GO

As you recall from the previous chapter, I learned to budget and save money at a young age. While you might think that it is a good thing to teach your kids while they're young to prepare them for adulthood, the harsh reality was that I learned these concepts out of survival mode! I did not learn them out of abundance. The devil used my mother's teaching moment as a way to make me believe that my provision was not possible.

I became so afraid of not having enough or not being able to purchase what I wanted that I was afraid to spend any amount of money. If this isn't poverty, then I don't know what is! Think about it like this: if I live paycheck to paycheck, then I'm living in poverty…and if I have more than enough and don't spend it, then I am *still* living in poverty! Wow! Did you catch that? Either way, there is a feeling of void and lack.

Holding on to things can be just as detrimental as giving them away (as in spending with no self-control or spending what you don't have). Sometimes, we hold on to our ideas, dreams, goals, and plans for so long that we stay stuck in a vicious cycle and continue to lack *purpose* in our lives. We never step out of our comfort zones or pursue what's next because of the fear of not having everything we need to succeed.

I want to take you through my experience as a teenager and young adult. I would often find myself going grocery shopping and purchasing the lowest priced items. I gave the example at the beginning of the book about choosing food that may be only a few cents cheaper but getting less for the price. I truly believed that this was "in my budget," but I hadn't yet discovered that there is no "budget" in God.

THE FRESHMAN YEAR CHRONICLES

When it came to shopping for clothes, I would immediately go to the clearance rack or look for the lowest priced items since they were more affordable. There is nothing wrong with being a good steward of your money and finding a great sale; however, I was living with a spirit of poverty, looking for the cheapest deal because I felt like I was limited. Let me paint this picture for you. As a teenager, I was embarking on a new journey. I was going to high school, and all of my friends were going to a different high school because we had moved to a different area. I didn't know anyone, and I would not only be the "new girl," but I would also be a freshman. We all know that you have to be "fly" as a freshman, otherwise you get picked on.

My mother told me that we were going to go clothes shopping for the new school year, and I was *excited!* I just *knew* that I would enter high school in *style* and that I would *not* look like a freshman. We went to J.C. Penney (it was popping back in the day), and we barely bought any outfits. I say barely because I *thought* I was getting a whole new wardrobe, but that was not the case. I think I got two shirts and two pairs of jeans. That was it! My hopes of fitting in were crushed. This meant I would also be wearing all old things from junior high school. I was reminded once again that I had limited access and that we could not afford much.

The spirit of poverty had taught me to accept everything "less than" because I didn't deserve better. As mentioned, poverty is a mentality and it causes us to have low self-esteem, to settle for *less than*, and to believe that we can never accomplish anything great in life. The freshman year chronicles made me feel "less than" because I couldn't afford clothes like the other kids.

I wasn't concerned about having name brand clothes, but couldn't I at least have had enough outfits to get me through a whole week of school? This experience helped to shape my identity and to associate myself with lack. Shopping for clothes became a tedious task for me, as I would often talk myself out of buying things with a thought process that went something like this: *"Well, I don't really need this. I mean, it's cute, but I can use that money to buy something else, like toiletries, or to pay a bill."* Some of you reading this book can relate to this behavior and perhaps some of you would have actually purchased the item, even though you couldn't afford it.

THE WAR IN YOUR HEAD

We can be so used to lack that we talk ourselves out of the *promise* of God. *God has promised that we are to experience heaven on earth, lacking nothing, and living an abundant life of freedom from lack. He has promised that HE shall provide ALL of our needs* (**Philippians 4:19** and **John 10:10**). What I am saying is that if you've worked hard, earned the money, paid your tithes, and paid your bills, then you deserve to treat yourself, especially if you are in need of new clothes. There is nothing wrong with heeding to wisdom in not spending what you don't have or don't really need. The Lord has promised to provide ALL of our needs and that we would lack nothing (**Matthew 6:28-33** and **Philippians 4:19**).

> There comes a time where the war in your head should not be the war in your hand!

We have to check our thoughts and put them into order. **2 Corinthians 10:5**: *"Casting down imaginations, and every high thing that exalteth itself against the knowledge of God and bringing into captivity every thought to the obedience of Christ."* We have to open our spiritual eyes to see ourselves the way the Lord sees us. All you have to do is ask Him.

We have to know that it is by God's grace (unmerited favor) that we are deserving and worthy of the necessary things for survival and also of the things we desire, according to His will. Why settle for something less when we have been created by default to have everything we need? The Word of God says that *"My God shall supply all of your needs according to his riches in Christ Jesus"* (**Philippians 4:19**). Our daddy God, our Father, has given us everything that He has and everything that He owns. Here are a few Scriptures that remind us that God owns everything…and what *He* owns, *we* own.

- **Psalm 50:10:** *"For every beast of the forest is mine and the cattle upon a thousand hills."*

- **John 1:3:** *"All things were made by him and without him, not anything was made."*

- **Colossians 1:6:** *"For by him all things created, that are in heaven and that in earth, visible and invisible, whether they be thrones, dominions or principalities or powers, all things were created by him and for him."*

- **Romans 8:16-17:** *"The Spirit itself beareth witness with our spirit, that we are the children of God: And if children, then heirs; heirs of God, and joint-heirs with Christ; if so be that we suffer with him, that we may be also glorified together."*

- **Ephesians 2:6:** *"And hath raised us up together and made us sit together in heavenly places in Christ Jesus."*

We are created to overcome every destructive power that keeps us in the bondage of poverty. The Lord has given us everything we need, and He gives us His favor (grace) for the things that we want. The type of relationship we have with our "wants" versus our "needs" can lead to a distorted view of God's grace. We can get mixed signals of who God *is* and who we *expect* Him to be.

"NO" CAN BE AN ANSWER TO PRAYER

Sometimes, God does miraculous things in our lives and answers our prayers quickly; and other times, we have to be patient and wait. I believe that God allows things to happen in our lives to show us that He is in control and that *He* has to be our *SOURCE for everything!* Otherwise, we fall into a deep pit that the devil dug just for us, so that he could bury us along with our dreams and our purpose. When this happens, our passion for life also dies.

When I think about poverty, I think about the *fear* of poverty. The fear behind poverty became a stumbling block in my life. It showed up in every area of my life, preventing me from having good and healthy friendships, family relationships, romantic relationships, careers, finances, and emotions. This mentality led to constant torment that would make me feel like I did not deserve to live a better life outside of what I knew.

I truly believe that once a person's mind is shifted to believing that they are not worthy, then the devil uses their emotions to change their behavior. Mental poverty is directly connected to and influenced by our emotions. The enemy attempts to lock us up in our own thoughts, and every attempt opens up another door which is at the seat of our emotions.

> Our behavior changes for the worse when we lose the battle between our sanity and our emotions.

QUESTIONS FOR REFLECTION

- *Growing up, did you feel like there were things that you could not have and that you had to go without because there wasn't enough money? How did it affect your perception of yourself?*

- *Do you feel that defaulting to the sale rack or clearance section comes from a poverty mindset, or do you see it as being a good steward of your resources?*

CHAPTER 4

EMOTIONAL POVERTY: TRAUMATIC EMOTIONS

At the seat of our emotions lies a series of internal reactions that are impacted by some form of trauma. Trauma in our lives opens the door to how we react and respond to situations. Trauma is spearheaded by fear, and fear causes disorder in our emotions. In order to understand how poverty affects our emotional health, we must first understand emotions. According to Merriam Webster, "emotion" is "*1. A conscious mental reaching (such as anger or fear) subjectively experienced as a strong feeling usually directed towards a specific object and typically accompanied by physiological and behavioral changes in the body. 2. A state of feeling. 3. The affective aspect of consciousness: feeling.*"

OUT OF BALANCE

Our emotions are the outward expression of our mental health. I'm no expert at brain health but what I do know is that once the brain receives a thought, an image is created and then a signal is directed to assign this thought to a reaction. I guess this is where we get the phrase, *"for every action, there is a RE-action."*

While researching how our brain works, I learned that psychologists say that we have six basic emotions: happiness, anger, sadness, fear, surprise, and disgust. Often, we experience some or all of these emotions at the same time. The goal should be to experience one emotion at a time, but the truth of the matter is, the devil hits us so hard back to back that our emotions can be all over the place. Have you ever met an emotionally unstable person? If so, don't be quick to judge. It could be that their emotions are out of balance due to fear and trauma, and they don't know how to get them back in order.

I am reminded of one of my favorite Scriptures that has been keeping my mind and emotions intact. **Isaiah 26:3**: *"Thou wilt keep him in perfect peace whose mind is stayed on thee because he trusteth in thee."* In other words, if we keep our eyes, our trust, our faith, and our vision on the Lord Jesus Christ, then HE will keep us in perfect peace.

In the Strong's Concordance, the word *"perfect"* in the Bible means *"maturity"* and the word *"peace"* means *"nothing broken, nothing missing."* The Lord will make sure that we have stability over our emotions and every transaction that happens in our minds. The enemy constantly plants images or thoughts in our minds, which are contrary to what God is saying *to* us and saying *about* us.

THE DANGER OF DISTORTED VISION

What happens when our vision is distorted and we can't see past our circumstances? How do we respond to the mental anguish that continues to play over and over in our minds? How do we see past the lie that tells us that we are not worthy of God's love? Is it because we live a reckless and unsubmitted life, that God is mad at us and wants nothing to do with us? At some point, we have all experienced circumstances that causes us to be confused about the love of the Father. The lies of the enemy deposit themselves into our emotions and infiltrate our emotional bank while withdrawing our self-esteem savings.

The thought of not having enough, for me, turned into a reactional thought pattern and feeling that I was "not good enough for anything or anybody." This reaction wasn't just a branch on a tree that one day appeared out of nowhere—it was deeply rooted in my mother's womb.

MY STORY

I was told that once my mother found out that she was pregnant with me, my father did not believe that I was his child, so he didn't want anything to do with me. After some time, my mother met my sister's father. They got married and then had my little sister. Her father was the only father I knew; so as far as I was concerned, he was my father. I remember him as fun, loving, and kind, and he protected me from the kids on the block. I don't remember him ever being angry or yelling, and he was the best representation of a good father. When I was about seven or eight years old, my mother and stepfather divorced, and my mother became a single parent, raising two girls on her own.

I remember my mother being very rigid, with a lot of "do's and don'ts," which birthed a high level of perfectionism in my life. As a child, I learned to follow orders, knowing that I didn't have a say in the matter and that I had better not mess anything up because my mother would be highly disappointed in me. As a result, I learned very early on that the only way to feel "loved" was to get my mother's approval. If she didn't approve, I didn't feel loved.

This rigid lifestyle taught me to suppress my emotions. I don't remember getting many hugs or words of affirmation such as *"You are beautiful," "It's okay if you mess up,"* or *"Good job."* Don't get me wrong. My mother was, and still is, sweet and pleasant. She congratulated me and supported me by attending my award ceremonies, step shows, and graduations. However, growing up, you deal with many emotional changes, and you find it very difficult to express what's going on with you on the inside.

WORDS HAVE POWER

There were not many opportunities where I was allowed to fully express myself; and when I tried to open up, I was shut down. I remember telling my mama one time that we needed to go to counseling. I had so much going on mentally and emotionally that I didn't know how to take control and manage it all. My mother listened to me and said, *"Okay,"* but nothing happened. I also remember a time where I tried to open up, and my mother said something like, *"Shut up, and go to your room. I don't want to hear it."* Words truly have power in them (**Proverbs 18:21**). These words were like ripping off a Band-Aid and pouring salt into the wound. I was already dealing with rejection and abandonment from my father; and now, I felt like an orphan.

Words have the power to either build you up (life) or tear you down (death). We must be careful of what we say and how we speak to children, because it causes even more confusion and disruption in the development of their identities.

As an adult, the Lord has shown me that my mother loved me; but being a single mom raising two girls, she just didn't know how to handle certain situations. She was not fully equipped with the tools, patience, and wisdom that she needed in order to help me navigate through life. I don't fault her, because I realize that she was only doing the best she knew how to do, based on what she was taught from her upbringing. As the older generation says, *"Children don't come with a book."*

Oftentimes, parents are learning as they go—but they have to understand that every child is different and every child learns, behaves, and receives love differently. If there was one cookie-cutter recipe for every individual, then we would all be perfect, and we wouldn't have a purpose in life. Unfortunately, most of us grow up in dysfunctional homes, adapting learned behaviors that we think are healthy and passing them down from generation to generation.

SIFTED LIKE WHEAT

Dysfunction breeds an environment and creates an opportunity for the opportunist, which is the devil. He is the *"thief in the night,"* and he *"comes only to steal, to kill, and to destroy"* (**John 10:10**). The enemy barged into my life and took whatever he wanted. I mean, geez, give me a break. I was only a child. The devil has an agenda, and his agenda is to destroy anything and everything that *looks like God.* We are created in the image of God. We are His children…and the devil can't stand it (**Genesis 1:26**).

The devil is our enemy, and he will go all out to destroy us regardless of sex, age, religion, beliefs, or career. He is not here to play games; he is here to KILL US, both spiritually and physically. The devil saw an opportunity in my life to *"sift me as wheat,"* as the Bible puts it in **Luke 22:31**.

Sifting wheat is a two-step process by which the edible part of the wheat is separated from the grain. The first step is called "threshing," and it is the process of sifting. The chaff (dry scaly protective casing of the seed) is loosened from the edible grain. There are machines that do this now, but the old-fashioned way was to spread the wheat on the floor, which was made from stone, concrete, or tamped earth, and then to beat it with a flail.

The flail is a threshing tool that consists of a wooden staff with a short heavy stick hanging from it. Farmers would hit the wheat repeatedly to knock off the edible grain. The second process is called "winnowing," and this is where the loosened chaff (protective casing) is removed from the grain. Winnowing was done by throwing the grain in the air, where the lighter chaff is blown off and the heavier grain falls back to the ground, separating the grain from the straw.

This sifting process is lengthy and deep. The devil continues to beat us and shake us over and over again with tragic circumstances, until we fall off and are removed from God's protection and guidance. His goal is to remove us (the grain) from the Father (the straw). He wants us to deny the power of Jesus in our lives so that we are powerless, despite the fact that the Lord gave us dominion and power over everything (**Luke 10:19** and **Genesis 1:28**).

WALKING IT OUT

I thank God that my mother did not abort me in the womb. Regardless of the initial rejection from my biological father, my heavenly Father did not reject me. In fact, from the moment I was conceived, the Lord stood up on my behalf. He knit me together in my mother's womb. He already had a plan and a purpose for my life, and He predestined me for greatness to do good works (**Psalm 139:13**, **Jeremiah 29:11**, and **Ephesians 2:10**).

Circumstances will either hinder you or push you further into walking out your destiny. As the story continues, I was just a child growing up in dysfunction, learning the ropes of the game. I became very fearful, intimidated, timid (something that those who know me well would find difficult to believe), a perfectionist, and very judgmental. I learned the power of hiding my emotions. From the view through my lens, I learned that there was no one to help me, I didn't have a voice, and no one cared about me. I hid my true self and how God created me to be, because I did not have the support to tell me that I could be myself and express my gifts and talents. All of these doors opened up in my life as multiple entry points that the devil used to keep me bound in poverty.

Since we are discussing the spirit of poverty, it is important to see that there are other spirits that keep us bound to poverty. These spirits I have briefly discussed in which you may see that they have also operated in your life. I dealt with the spirits of rejection (including self-rejection), abandonment, low self-esteem, hopelessness, and the orphan spirit. As a result, I became angry, resentful, and depressed in middle school, which is the exact opposite of who I am today. In addition, I had a mother wound, and I also had a father wound. I was left to defend and protect myself, by any means necessary.

SABOTAGING THE BLESSING

Defending and isolating yourself is a protective mechanism that operates out of a spirit of pride.

Any time you feel like you can *"do life"* on your own and you *"don't need nobody,"* then you are dealing with pride. And unfortunately, pride leads to destruction and more chaos in our lives. **Proverbs 16:18** *"Pride goeth before destruction, and a haughty spirit before a fall."* Pride causes us to be rebellious and do the opposite of what God is trying to do in our lives.

> We sabotage our blessings because of our unwillingness to change our stubborn ways.

If there is any area in your life where you have fallen away from God, or nothing seems to be going right—check your heart's posture and see if the spirit of pride is lingering somewhere. Every spirit is attached to another spirit, and it catches you up in a web of chaos.

The depths of Satan's plans and devices run deeper than you can imagine. The devil wasn't just interested in causing me to shed a few tears, feel sorry for myself, or wonder why my mother and father didn't love me. He wanted to control my emotions. Satan wanted to make sure that I never learned who I was in the Lord or of the mighty power that was my inheritance. He came to steal my joy, so that my strength in God would be lost. Why? Because *"the joy of the Lord is our strength"* (**Nehemiah 8:10**).

Once the joy is lost, any circumstance can come blow your house down (death). As a matter of fact, in high school, the devil revisited me and began to "tell me" about myself. He kept telling me that no one cared about me…that my mother loved my sister more…that my daddy didn't want me…that I was ugly…that I was a failure. He said to me, *"No one cares about you. You're a nobody, so you might as well kill yourself."* He said it, and I believed it.

I was overwhelmed with school, my emotions, and my life in general. I didn't have an older sibling or relatives that I could talk to, and I felt defeated and hopeless. One particular day while I was in the shower, I silently cried, with big huge tears rolling down my face. I was thinking that life was too much, and I couldn't go another day. I was sad, hopeless, alone, and confused. I didn't understand why I felt the way I did, and I was afraid to express this to my mother. I heard a small, calm voice that said, *"Kill yourself, and all of this will go away."*

I remember this day like it was yesterday, and I've only shared this with a few people. I heard the voice of the one that was trying to "sift me as wheat." I thought of all the possible ways to kill myself at that moment, and the only thing that I could think of was to choke myself to death. Funny but not funny. This is the part where common sense kicked in! I was like, *"Hold up. That doesn't even make sense. How are you going to choke yourself to death? At some point, the muscles in your hands will lose their grip, and you're not going to be very successful."*

I laughed and thought, *"Devil, that's just stupid. It doesn't even make sense."* After that, I heard a louder voice say, *"If you kill yourself, then everyone is going to be sad."* My emotions were triggered, and I thought about how my family would be so sad and unable to live their lives because of my death. I didn't want anyone to be sad or to feel pain like I did, so I decided that there was a purpose for my life. As I know now, the louder voice was the Holy Spirit of God. He was my deliverer, my defender, and my comforter. Even though I did not have a relationship with the Lord, I knew who He was, and I knew the difference between good and evil. God's word states (paraphrased) that *"His sheep hear His voice. They follow Him and they resist any stranger, for they will not follow a stranger"* (**John 10: 5, 27**). From that day forth, I haven't thought about committing suicide because God showed me that HE loves me!

WORTHY OF THE PROMISE

The devil likes to play mind games with us and with our emotions. He tried to convince me that I was better off dead and that there was no purpose for my life. I'm here to tell you that *everyone* has a purpose. We are all fully fashioned and equipped for good works and to change the lives of others. We are worthy of His promises and through the blood of Jesus, He has set us free.

The Holy Spirit lives on the inside of each and every one of us; and just as He spoke to me that day, He will also speak to you. I didn't attend church in high school; but as a child, I used to go to Vacation Bible School during the summer and church on Sundays, so I learned the difference between right and wrong. I had never heard God's voice before, but I thank God that His roots were planted and established in the inside of me when He created me. If the Lord had not spoken to me that day, I believe that my family would have lived with consistent stagnation, limitations, and unfruitful lives.

When the Lord created us, He gave us the fruits of the Holy Spirit and one of them is joy (**Galatians 5:22**). I have been a bundle of joy, my mama tells me, since birth. I believe I have been sent to the Earth to bring joy to the world. The devil can try to steal your joy, but he has to flee when you resist him. When you resist him, you literally engage him. You declare *war* against him. And how do you wage war? You use the Word of God! I didn't have the Word in me at that time, but the Holy Spirit spoke the Word into my mind and that was *"You shall live and not die; there is a plan and purpose for your life"* (**Proverbs 118:17**).

The poverty mindset is one that shows up in your mind, your will, and your intellect. It manifests itself with the spirit of death (can be both natural and spiritual death). The spirit of death is deeply rooted in poverty, and it comes to kill our dreams, our purpose, and our destiny. In our society, we are taught to "Suck it up. Put on your big girl or your big boy drawers. Keep it moving." Unfortunately, we are all living in dysfunction, and we normalize it because we are unaware of how to combat it.

Our emotions can take us "up and away" from God's purpose and plans for our lives. Satan can take full advantage of us if he can get into our mind and get to the seat of our emotions. The Bible puts it like this: *"Lest Satan should get an advantage of us: for we are not ignorant of his devices"* (**2 Corinthians 2:11**). Once the enemy's plans have been exposed, you will start to see through a different lens. You will exchange *your* lens for *God's* lens, and you will notice the devil using the same patterns and tricks over and over again. If you catch on to his game, he'll try to change the rules. He'll come at you from a different angle but use the same tactics. Ha! The devil is not very creative, because he is not the creator of anything…God is! But be aware, because once Satan has your mind and takes over your emotions, he will take his throne right to the seat of your relationships.

QUESTIONS FOR REFLECTION

- *How was communication modeled in your home growing up? Did you observe healthy dialogue? Were the members of the family encouraged to express their thoughts and feelings?*

- *How did the dynamics from your home affect you as an adult? If you are a parent, do you encourage your children to express their emotions? Do you and your partner/significant other prioritize good communication?*

CHAPTER 5

RELATIONSHIP POVERTY

When you feel like you are lacking in a certain area of your life, you try to hold on to everything you have, including your relationships.

IN THE BEGINNING...

From the beginning, the devil has been infatuated with destroying relationships. In the Garden of Eden, Satan convinced Eve to eat from the forbidden tree that caused her to tempt her husband and then caused them to both be ashamed. There was a separation between mankind and God, and there was now also discord between Adam and Eve!

Can you imagine the conversation they had after this incident occurred? Adam blamed Eve for his downfall. He told God that, *"It was the woman! She gave me the fruit!"* (**Genesis 3:12**) and *that* was why he disobeyed God. Here we see fear and self-condemnation, plus the blame game. Can you imagine if your spouse threw you under the bus for something that they were supposed to be in charge of? Do you see how the crime that they committed *together* was sin?

Sin separated us from having a relationship and being in right standing with God. The fall of man was devastating…but thank God for Jesus who died for us and set us free from this curse! The salvation of Jesus permits us to be in right relationship with God because of His grace and mercy. *"For by grace are ye saved through faith; and that not of yourselves: it is the gift of God: Not of works, lest any man should boast"* (**Ephesians 2:8-9**).

We can see that Satan has a deep hatred for relationships and will go above and beyond, working overtime, to destroy God's original design—His creation. Adam and Eve were in perfect harmony and peace with God; they had a covenant relationship with the Father. And although we see the theme of division in the Book of Genesis, it did not start there. See, prior to Satan being cast down to earth, he was in heaven with the other angels.

Let me give you a little background on Satan. Satan's name was Lucifer, and he was the *"Son of the morning"* (**Isaiah 14:12**). Lucifer was the *"anointed cherub, adorned with every precious jewel, the model of perfection, full of wisdom and beauty"* (**Ezekiel 28:12-14**). He had everything that he needed, but his *pride* got the best of him and caused him to think that he could overthrow God. **Isaiah 14:13-14** tells us of the conversation that took place in his heart:

> *"For thou hast said in thine heart, I will ascend into heaven, I will exalt my throne above the stars of God: I will sit also upon the mount of the congregation, in the sides of the north: I will ascend above the heights of the clouds; I will be like the most High."*

Lucifer compared himself to God, and he couldn't stand the thought of being second best. He convinced one third of the angels to join him in his mission of rebellion against God (**Revelation 12:4**). Can you imagine the life that he and all of the angels had up there in heaven? They had everything! They didn't have to worry about pain, sorrow, sickness…I often wonder how he convinced those angels to join him? Why did they choose to follow him? And what about the other angels? I would think they were like siblings. I can only imagine the other angels like, *"Dude! What's your issue? You need to calm down and get yourself together!"* But Lucifer messed around and got kicked out of heaven…and he lost his name, his title, and his position.

Like the devil, many of us become dissatisfied with our position, and we allow our pride to make decisions that disrupt what God is doing in our lives. The poverty mentality can either cause us to push healthy relationships away (isolation), hold on to toxic relationships (denial), or both. I have been on both sides of the spectrum.

RELATIONSHIP POVERTY

Growing up, I never cared about being part of the "in crowd." I knew that I was different, and I always felt like an outcast. I was smart, on the honor roll, had morals and standards…but I was missing something. I was missing the love of my parents. Remember, my father left me before I was even born, and my mother was busy working as a single parent. In addition, my sister and I were like night and day. We are three and a half years apart, and I am the oldest. Growing up, it seemed as though my mother expected more out of me than she expected out of my sister, and I would often get into trouble for things that she did. This led to the idea that my mama loved her more and didn't care about me.

I remember one particular incident where my sister put candy wrappers in the toilet, and it got clogged. My mother blamed my cousin and I, saying, *"She couldn't have done that."* For the life of my mother, she just couldn't put the blame on the baby! No, not her baby! My sister could have gotten away with murder, and my mother would still blame me as the criminal. I believe that this division between my parents and then with my sister led me to fall into a deeper lie which told me that no one cared about me or was there to protect me.

I longed for love, attention, and affirmation. *Anything* to let me know that I was worthy of love. Relationship poverty expresses itself as a need or desire that is not being met. What happens if a need is not being met? When my need for love and affection was not met, I hid

> *When you don't feel loved, you sit in a position of abandonment.*

my emotions, stayed quiet, and isolated myself. I entered into romantic relationships with men who were also broken, looking for validation in my identity, only to fall into a deeper ditch which created an even bigger void.

THE POSITION OF ABANDONMENT

Abandonment robs us of our freedom to trust in *anyone*…including God Himself. In my case, I first recognized abandonment in my family line. I was in my own world, and I gravitated to a tsunami lifestyle of dysfunctional relationships. I learned to depend on myself, feeling like Ms. Independent. I didn't know this at the time, but I was trying to fill a void in my life that had been established before I was born. God's original design is for family unity. He never intended for us to live in dysfunction. Merriam-Webster defines dysfunction as:

1. *impaired or abnormal functioning (gastrointestinal dysfunction),*

2. *abnormal or unhealthy interpersonal behavior or interaction within a group (family dysfunction)*

The first definition intrigued me, and I took a closer look. Merriam-Webster included the gastrointestinal (GI) tract to describe dysfunction. That's powerful. The Holy Spirit revealed to me that the GI tract is responsible for ingesting food, digesting it, and making it available for the nourishment of our bodies. It is also where our immune system starts. In order to navigate through life and to be immune to the plans, plots, and schemes of our adversary—the devil—we must have a healthy, functioning natural immune system.

DOING LIFE TOGETHER

The second definition is more self-explanatory, and it shows that there can be abnormal interaction and disorder within our family dynamics. Family is important to God. He created us to be in perfect harmony with Him but also to be in perfect harmony with our family! Despite our differences, we can all come together for a bigger purpose, which is to destroy the works of the devil. Unity in the family builds a legacy for generations to come!

We must learn how to "do life together," with *all* of the members of our family. Sounds simple right? Our family dynamics are the roots that shapes our beliefs, our personalities, our actions, and our identity. It also determines how we view and function in other relationships. Many times, we take on the characteristics of our parents, believing that their way of living is normal, when it is actually abnormal and unhealthy. Abnormal behaviors and patterns are considered dysfunctional. It's not until we interact with other individuals outside of our family and through the Word of God that we learn the difference between dysfunction and function.

The Lord has given us the blueprints for healthy relationships; however, once we adapt to and normalize dysfunctional living, a door of desensitization is opened to the mental, emotional, and physical state of health for each one of our family members. It is only when we have a divine encounter with the power of God's love that we begin to see the functions of dysfunction. If our definition of family and love is distorted, then we have a misconception about the love that comes from our Heavenly Father!

I was broken as a child, and I didn't realize the impact that it had on me in my adulthood. I didn't feel love from my natural father, and I resented him. But through God's grace, the Lord used my mother to help me learn to love him unconditionally and to fully forgive him. The absence of a father can cause you to look for love in all the wrong places.

On the other hand, I experienced the lack of love from my mother which was based on *what my needs were, not necessarily what she could provide.* The relationship strain that I had from rejection hindered my relationships and affected my ability to trust people. I became a people-pleaser, looking for affirmations and the approval of man. I wanted my mother to be proud of me, give me attention, and show me love.

THE INTIMIDATION FACTOR

I made sure that I had the best grades. I cleaned the house regularly, and I decided not to be that "rebellious teenager." I consulted my mother on every decision in my life and became a perfectionist—afraid to mess up and make the wrong decisions. As a result, I became double-minded and had difficulty making decisions, especially when I had too many options on the table. As I grew up, the Lord dealt with me on this issue, and I realized that I would have been more stable in my thoughts had my mother just told me that it was okay to make a mistake and that she loved me unconditionally.

Earlier, I gave you some insight into my mother, and how she was very rigid. I never saw her cry, and I never saw her emotions. She was a tough cookie on the outside, but I knew deep down that she had a soft interior. It was the tough outer layer where I indirectly learned to "chin up" and to suppress my emotions. This suppression led to the inability to express myself in a healthy way. I was afraid to speak up for myself. I felt inferior and intimidated, especially by those in a position of authority over my career, my schooling, and my family. I dealt with the mental anguish of low self-esteem, and my friendships suffered as well. Looking back on my past, I know now that I was a hot mess, completely dysfunctional, and wrong in how I treated my friends. I thought I was "just being me," but clearly, I was in the wrong.

In high school, my best friend and I were inseparable. We joined the same activities, hung out every day, and even worked the same jobs together. But I had a problem. I would bottle up stress and frustrations, suppress my emotions, isolate myself…and if someone said something that I did not like or that struck a nerve, I would "snap, crackle, and pop." I was a ticking time bomb, ready to go off at any minute. This occurred in high school but also when we went to college together.

When I was stressed, I would be quiet for days, not speaking to or even acknowledging my best friend, with whom I shared a dorm room. I would just go mute without an explanation. All I knew was that I needed time to myself to figure it out. To this day, it still amazes me that she remained my friend all that time. She rationalized it by saying, *"that's just Stefani,"* but in reality, it was dysfunctional and abusive to her. She didn't deserve to be treated like that, and I definitely wasn't being a friend. Eventually, my isolation led to the end of our friendship.

There's more to the story, but the root of it all was a lack of someone understanding my struggles. No one had ever taught me how to deal with the stressors of life or how to let go of my internal frustrations effectively.

I never saw any examples of healthy interaction modeled by my mother, my family, nor my friend.

DYSFUNCTION LOVES DYSFUNCTION

The devil loves connecting dysfunctional people to other dysfunctional people. Two wrongs don't make a right, and two dysfunctional people can't help each other out of dysfunction. I was expecting my friend to provide the love, attention, and affirmation that I did not receive from my parents. The solution, as I saw it, was having someone support me by simply asking, *"How are you doing?"*, *"Are you okay, Stef?"*, or *"How are you feeling today?"* I thought that if my parents were not there for me, then at least my best friend should be there.

The truth of the matter was, my friend couldn't help me either. She was just as dysfunctional as I was, and she simply didn't know how to help. In her defense, I never expressed what was wrong with me and what I needed from her, so that she could show her support.

> We expect people to know our needs and wants, but people are not mind readers, and everyone has a different way of providing love and support.

Some of us need words of affirmation and encouragement, while others need to spend quality time or receive gifts as a demonstration of support and appreciation.

The devil wants us to believe that people should be able to handle our dysfunction, but that is a lie. Some people are graced to handle one area, and others are graced to handle another area because they have already mastered that area in their own lives. Be assured that the Lord will expose the dysfunctions in your life, and He will lead you to the people who can help you uproot, rebuild, and cultivate healthy functional relationships.

SISTER SISTER

Dysfunction as a result of poverty can also express itself through your siblings. My relationship with my younger sister, Sharon, was not really a relationship at all. We were like night and day, fighting constantly, and never really communicating with one another. As children, we would play games with one another but never really had that "sisterhood bond." I felt that my mother played favorites, mainly because she was the baby, and my mother was also the baby of her siblings. My name was always the first name to be called on if something happened.

Showing favoritism to one child over the other is another form of dysfunction. It produces chaos, confusion, and division, because the affected child no longer feels protected by the parent. It can create a barrier to healthy relationships not only between siblings, but also in other relationships later on in life. I was never upset or jealous of Sharon, but I was upset with my mother for not being there for me like she was with her. I quickly learned that my sister was very sensitive, and my mother babied her, but maybe this was because my mother was also the baby out of her siblings. We produce the fruit that has been given to us!

As my sister and I got older, we went to the same university, lived in the same dorm, then lived only fifteen minutes away from each other… and *still* never had a relationship. We didn't know what sisterhood was, and we were complete strangers.

College life is all about finding yourself and your purpose in life. As I was trying to find my purpose, I joined a non-Greek Christian sisterhood called Elogeme Adolphi Christian Sorority, Inc. This is where I learned the true definition of sisterhood and love. Sharon and I were like night and day; she enjoyed the club life, and I enjoyed the godly life. I didn't ask her to join the sisterhood with me because she was doing her own thing, and I didn't think that she would be interested. Later on, she wrote a book about her life, and I read the part that discussed sisterhood. She wanted a relationship with me; and when she saw that I joined this sorority, she couldn't fathom why I would embrace my new sisters and not my own biological sister.

After reading this book, I realized that I did not intentionally reject her; I was just trying to find my own way. And since she and I didn't have a relationship or connection with one another, we didn't know how to embrace our differences and incorporate each other into our own lives. I believe that we learned these dysfunctional behaviors through our family because we never saw true sisterhood with my mother and her siblings.

My mother is the youngest out of eight: she has four brothers and three sisters. They used to hang out when they were younger, and there were some siblings who had stronger bonds than others. The dynamics of their relationship changed as they got older. Growing up, I saw my mother and her sisters help each other out in times of crisis, but I didn't see them communicate well, encourage one another, or show affection to one another. What I observed was isolation, resentment, rejection, and abandonment.

THE SPIRIT OF ABANDONMENT

The devil does a fancy job of causing sibling rivalry by trapping us within the spirits of rejection and abandonment. He knows that if he can create tension and division between siblings, then he can open the door for other kinds of spirits to enter, such as pride and manipulation. The sibling rivalry in my life opened my heart to a deep, dark world of bondage that caused me to treat my sister poorly when we were younger. Although I wasn't upset or jealous of her, I was controlling and manipulative and didn't know it. I am not proud of it, but I'm also not that same person I used to be. I am going to share with you a family secret; and later, I'll explain why this is a family secret. As a child, I remember that we used to play our Super Nintendo video games every day. I took it upon myself to be in charge of the game, and I manipulated my sister by convincing her that I could win the board she was playing if she supplied me with cookies. Every time I lost, I would tell her that it was because *the cookies gave me energy, and I needed more.* This is funny now that I look back on it, but it was actually the devil working in my ego and shaping my identity. I guess this gave me the position to be heard or to be needed.

QUEEN OF THE UNIVERSE

Any time Sharon asked me to do something for her, I would make her say, *"Can I have _____, Stefani, Queen of the Universe?"* How audacious of me, right? I mean, what gave me the right to think that I *owned* the universe and that my sister worked under my control and authority? I say that this is a family secret because it's in the family. No one knew about this nor did anyone talk about these things. I know that if I behaved in this manner, then someone else in my family's bloodline had to have acted like this at some point.

I never saw my mother do this specifically, but she made it known that she was the one in charge. These dysfunctional behaviors are generational curses, and every individual family member is prone to hide them without ever addressing the truth of the matter.

A MATTER OF THE HEART

The truth of the matter is that the manifestations of pride and manipulation are a matter of the heart.

Jeremiah 17:9: *"The heart is deceitful above all things and desperately wicked; who can know it?"*

Luke 6:45: *"A good man out of the good treasure of his heart bringeth forth that which is good; and an evil man out of the evil treasure of his heart bringeth forth that which is evil: for out of the abundance of the heart his mouth speaketh."*

In other words, the things that you say and do are a reflection of what's really in your heart. We cannot trust our own hearts because the issues of life are seated in our hearts.

Proverbs 4:23: *"Keep thy heart with all diligence; for out of it are the issues of life."*

In my case, I actually *believed* that it was okay for me to manipulate my little sister and make her bow down to me as if I was someone important.

Here's the revelation: *when you are left to fend for yourself, raise yourself, exalt, and affirm yourself because you didn't receive affirmation as a child, you become full of pride.* Pride take its seat in your heart, and it destroys your blood supply, which is the oxygen you need to live! It causes you to puff yourself up, making you feel grandiose, worthy, and necessary, while slowing sucking the life (purpose) out of the lives of those you are supposed to love.

Can you imagine how my sister must have felt when I only showed my love by controlling her? I can only imagine the damage I may have caused because of my own dysfunction and how it spilled into her future relationships. I thank God that I am no longer who I used to be and that God delivered me from that way of life and that way of thinking.

The enemy walked himself right into the journey of our sisterhood. He thought he would destroy our relationship forever, but the Lord had another plan. See, Sharon and I couldn't have a healthy relationship because we were looking through the lens that was provided to us at birth. We only did what we saw and what we were taught.

It's unfortunate that we, particularly as a Black family, do not know how to support one another in love. Everyone wants their side of the story heard, and they have this "woe is me" and "no one understands me" mentality. Our past hurts, pains, and disappointments shape our perspectives and our expectations of each other. But, if we truly sit down, intentionally listen and talk to our siblings about our needs and how we like to be supported, without judgment, then we will see breakthroughs in our families.

THE BATTLE FOR THE FAMILY

The first place the enemy attacks is our family. He did this with the first family: Adam, Eve, and their children, Cain and Abel, which eventually led us to Jesus. The Bible says that Cain killed his brother, Abel, because of jealousy (**Genesis 4:1-8**). This is not a new topic! It's a sin that has been passed down from generation to generation. The devil's goal is for us to destroy each other so that we destroy our families. Why? Because the Lord established His covenant with us through family.

The devil couldn't fathom how Jesus could still have power on earth while He was in heaven. It was because Jesus gave us His Holy Spirit to advance the Kingdom of God and destroy the kingdom of darkness

(**John 14:15-16** and **1 John 3:8**). When we accept Jesus as our Lord and Savior (**Romans 10:9**), we are filled with the Holy Ghost (**Acts 1:8**). We are earthly vessels filled with the power to depopulate hell and advance the Kingdom of God. The Lord has given us all power over the enemy (**Luke 10:19**), and we have the power to restore broken fellowship with our parents and siblings. I want to encourage you not to give up on your family. We need each other to survive.

I want you to know that the Lord takes pleasure in seeing families reunite! It is His will that we be reconciled to one another. God still has a plan for siblings. And although my sister and I didn't see eye to eye, I desired to be reconciled with her. I longed for the day that we would be reunited and that we could "do life" together. I had spiritual sisters, but I wanted the bond that we were supposed to have had from the beginning. Throughout the years, I would pray that God would show my sister her identity in HIM, during a process where I was learning my identity in Jesus Christ.

About ten years later, my sister gave her life to Christ and fully submitted to His will. The Lord brought us together in unity as a result of my prayer life! I was overjoyed because I wanted her to experience the deliverance and freedom that I had experienced. Rebuilding our relationship was not at all easy. There were times during our journey where I didn't open up and share things with her, either because she offended me by something she assumed about me, or because I felt like she totally dismissed my feelings when I would try to express myself. I felt like she just didn't know the "new" Stefani, and she didn't know me as a person, outside of her sister.

I didn't trust my sister with my feelings, thoughts, or plans, and this caused me to build up a wall in my heart. Every time my sister and I talked, we would get into a disagreement, not knowing how to "agree to disagree" and keep it moving. I started tuning her out because she didn't understand how I needed to be supported. She thought that the way she did things in her life was the way that I should do things in my life. Do you see how dysfunctional it is to expect something from someone but never discuss your expectations of that person in the relationship? We can all agree that at some point in our lives, we become disappointed with others and we cut off the relationship and communication…and *it is all because that person cannot fill our needs*. The poverty mentality rears its ugly head once again, sabotaging our relationships.

- It opens the door to trust issues.

- We build walls in our hearts as protective mechanisms from hurt.

- We dismiss the feelings of others.

- It prevents us from discovering our true identity.

The enemy's plan is to overload you with all of these spirits whose primary goal is to keep you stuck in dysfunctional patterns, so that you will isolate yourself and shut down the access to your heart. If the Lord is unable to access your heart and the issues of life that flow from it, then you'll never have access to His promises of deliverance, freedom, and life!

WALKING OUT THE SISTERHOOD

I want to conclude that the story between my sister and I is one for the books! Once my sister and I found our identities in Christ, the Lord worked on both of our hearts. Even though we had trust issues with one another, we still needed to "learn" each other and be sensitive to each other's needs. I continued to pray for the reconciliation in our relationship but didn't know that I would have to do some work.

One day at my cousin's house, we were having a family meeting, and my cousin mentioned that my sister had told him that she and I didn't feel like sisters; we felt more like friends. It was at this moment that the Lord pricked at my heart, and He overwhelmed me with His love. My heart was saddened that she felt that way because I had always yearned for true sisterhood with my blood sister and here it was…she didn't feel this way.

My eyes flooded with tears, and I apologized to her in front of everyone. I didn't care who saw me. At that moment, I knew I loved my sister, and I knew that *she loved me*. I went over to the couch to hug her, and we decided to discuss our feelings over dinner. We scheduled a dinner date;

and that day, we began to talk to one another. She didn't know how I felt and was not even aware that she offended me, and vice versa.

At the end of dinner, we agreed to be more open and aware of each other's needs, not judging one another, and learning how and why we respond a certain way to certain situations. I can honestly say that today, my sister is one of my biggest supporters. She loves me for who I am! She is my cheerleader, my encourager, and my corrector, and I love her the same way. God has restored our relationship, and we are walking out our sisterhood.

I was moved to share my personal testimony of sibling rivalry because whether or not you have siblings, you may have experienced some form of rivalry in your family. I want to add that when we have low self-worth and low self-esteem, and our essential needs are not being met, then all of our relationships suffer. We may not be aware of what is operating in our lives and why, but God has placed us in our specific families for a reason. We have to see past our own lens and ask God to show us from His lens how He sees each member of our family. I believe that once you see from the Lord's eyes, then you will be able to love each individual family member unconditionally.

THROUGH THE LENS OF THE FATHER

My personal prayer has been one where I ask the Lord to let me see people the way He sees them. This prayer is pure in nature, and it has allowed me to not be offended or hold a grudge, but to recognize the condition of their soul. I see my family and other individuals as human beings. I have learned that *the secret to winning at relationships is empathy*. Empathy is the ability to place myself in someone else's shoes, looking at their past, and seeing how poverty has robbed them of their identity. It is also looking at an individual through the lens of the Father.

We are told in **2 Corinthians 5:16** that we are to *"know no man by the flesh."* The only way to know him is to know him by the Spirit of God, in which God has given us His spirit (**1 Corinthians 2:12, 1 John 4:13,** and **2 Corinthians 5:5**).

QUESTIONS FOR REFLECTION

- *Did you grow up in what you would consider an emotionally stable environment? Were love and affection given freely and unconditionally?*

- *How has the emotional environment of the home that you grew up in affected you as an adult? Specifically, how has it affected your...*

  o relationships?

  o parenting decisions?

  o job and social interactions?

CHAPTER 6

ABANDONED BY THE FATHER: CHILD SUPPORT

Poverty robs you from learning the power of your family's purpose, especially when the head of the family unit is absent. The absence of the head of the family is the breeding ground for rejection and abandonment.

THE ROLE OF THE FATHER

When God placed Adam in the Garden of Eden, He made him the head of the household and put him in charge of the statutes of God. God established the role of the father when He said, *"Let us make man in our image..."* in **Genesis 1:26**. After the serpent tricked Eve into eating the forbidden fruit and giving it to her husband, they suddenly noticed that they were naked. Take note...it wasn't until *Adam* took a bite that they noticed that they were naked. This tells us that fathers have the ultimate responsibility for protecting the family and setting the course for the purpose of the family.

In this story, we don't know where Adam was or what he was doing, but what we *can* conclude is that Adam was not in his position. We see a similar trend in today's modern Black families where the fathers are not present. We now see single-parent homes where mothers have had to take on the responsibility of filling both parental roles. This may not be everyone's case but is was certainly my case.

Remember, I only knew my sister's father as my father, and he was my protector and my provider. He left when I was very young; but when I was about nine years old, my mother told me that I had a biological father and that he wanted to meet me. I was shocked, upset, sad, anxious, and confused. Later that night, I became very sad and started to cry because for me, that meant that the only father I had ever known would not be coming back and that there was someone new to take his place.

So many questions flooded my mind. Who would this new person be that was entering into my life? What did he look like? Did he have a lot of money? How come he decided to show up all of a sudden? Where had he been all this time? I had been so accustomed to our new way of living with just the three of us (my sister, my mother, and I), minding our own business, that I wasn't sure I wanted an additional person added to my life. One day, there was a knock on the door, and I finally met my biological father.

THE ORPHAN SPIRIT

I had dreamed of a light-skinned man with muscles and nice wavy hair. I don't know why I thought that but that's not what I got! My father was a stocky man, dark-skinned; and while he didn't have wavy hair, he *did* have a nice grade of hair. He came with gifts: clothes, a piggy bank, money, and a baby doll. Part of me was upset as I thought to myself, *"He doesn't even know me, because if he did, he wouldn't have brought me a baby doll!"* I was never into playing with baby dolls. It was nice of him to bring me those things, but I was still wondering why he decided to show up after all those years.

As time went on, I discovered that my father had two sons who were older than me. They would come over to my house, and we would go go-kart racing and have so much fun. They were super cool, and we all meshed well (unlike my sister and I). It was like being the same person and having the same personality in different bodies. I had very good times; but quickly learned of some dark areas and flaws in my father that I believe were highly connected to poverty, rejection, and abandonment. These areas presented themselves in every area of my life as strongholds.

My father would call and let me know that he was coming over to bring me some money. I was filled with joy, waiting for him to visit. I was like a kid, patiently waiting to go to the candy store or to Great America for my birthday. But time after time, he would say that he was on his way and wouldn't show up until three or four hours later. And sometimes, he would tell me that he couldn't give me the money because he needed to pay a bill or fix something on his car. This was the turning point in our relationship. Disappointment kicked in the door to let in the spirits of anger, resentment, rejection, and abandonment.

I couldn't stand a person who made promises, only to break them. I thought, *"Don't tell someone you're on your way and it takes you three hours when it should only take thirty minutes. And don't spend money that you promised to give to me. If that's the case, just let it be a surprise."*

This pattern shaped how I viewed my father, and it incubated and birthed more dysfunction in my life. I became so accustomed to being let down that I stopped having hope and trust in not only my father, but also in every person in my life. I learned to not fully trust people by putting another wall up in my heart.

The devil will find pathways to create environments of abandonment which influences our belief system and colors how we view our Father in heaven. It makes us believe that the Lord leaves us hopeless by abandoning us just as our natural fathers did. But this is a lie from the pit of hell. The Lord has promised us that he *"will never leave us nor forsake us"* and that *"when our mother and father forsake us that the Lord will take us up"* (**Deuteronomy 31:6**, **Hebrews 13:5**, and **Psalm 27:10**).

I didn't know about this promise over my life. I just knew that I was full of rejection, disappointment, and feelings of abandonment. In essence, I developed an "orphan spirit," feeling rejected, unprotected, and dealing with a lack of provision. My experiences trickled over into my romantic relationships with men. If someone told me that they would buy me something or wanted to do something nice for me, my response was, *"Right. Okay. I'll believe it when I see it."*

EXCUSES, EXCUSES, EXCUSES

The setup for the relationship that I had with my father seemed to follow me in every relationship that I had with a man. I always seemed to choose men who couldn't really advance me in life. They too dealt with the spirit of poverty. I remember one guy asking me what I wanted for Christmas. I never really asked the guys I dated for anything; but since my cross necklace had broken, I asked him for a new one.

When we got to the jewelry stand in the store, he complained that it cost too much. For heaven's sake, it was only $80 for a gold necklace! He was used to buying silver jewelry, and silver is cheaper. What really got to me was that he spent $100 on a diamond silver cross pendant for himself. I was completely blown away. I felt like this was a slap in the face and that boyfriend never had to worry about me asking him to buy me anything else again!

I dated another guy who had all the excuses, just like my father. He would say that he was on his way to visit me, then not show up for hours. His excuse was always, *"I got pulled over by the police," "I had a flat tire,"* or *"I had to go to the ER because my blood pressure was up."* Unfortunately, I stayed in these relationships far too long. I was looking to fill a void and had a need for someone to talk and make me feel special. These are relationships where a reflection of how *poverty is present in everyone* and how we *settle for less* actually reflects our image of the identity of our father, whether natural or heavenly.

The enemy is a thief, and he will steal our identity as a son or daughter in the Lord. He distorts the image of fatherhood, using our biological fathers as bait. My past experience with my biological father is not a reflection of the relationship I have with him today. In fact, the Lord has given me grace to extend grace and mercy to him. God used my mother as a conduit to bring light and revelation to my father's actions. She never talked badly about him or put him down. I vividly remember one day when she said to me, *"Stef, give your father a chance. I think he is doing the best that he knows how."* She had mercy and compassion for him. From that day forth, my attitude changed toward him. I chose to forgive him and release him from my expectations of who I thought he was and who he should be.

I give all glory to God, because I now have a good relationship with my father. My mother planted the seeds of grace, mercy, and compassion in my heart. The seeds were watered by my decision to forgive and release him, and the Lord gave the increase, which led to a good relationship. If we are willing to do the work, then surely, we will see the increase in our lives. *"I have planted, Apollos watered; but God gave the increase"* (**1 Corinthians 3:6**).

PROTECTING THE HEART

My relationship with my father and the choices that I have made in life could have gone south had my mother been negative and bitter about my father's absence. If I had never given him a chance, I would have grown up with anger, rage, bitterness, unforgiveness, and resentment. These spirits open the door to all kinds of illnesses and diseases, such as cancer, autoimmune disorders, high blood pressure, arthritis, and migraines. The Lord protected my heart, because that's what fathers do!

I can now say that my father and I are constantly building a healthy relationship. Relationships of any kind take time, and communication must always be the core foundation. You may have your individual likes and dislikes, but it doesn't mean that the other person has to have the same perspective. One thing that I have learned is that you have to make your expectations and communications clear. This means saying to a person, *"When you say this_____, I feel this_____."* This will help bring clarity to the other person and help them to effectively communicate with you.

If you don't try to understand where the other person is coming from and you keep pushing your way of doing things, then you will miss the opportunity to build a trustworthy and healthy relationship. The goal with any relationship is to empathize with others, put yourself in their shoes, and see beyond their past hurts, pains, and griefs. I promise, you will see life from a different angle. The door to the healing of my father wound was seeing him for who he was and not expecting anything, but instead realizing that he was only responding in the way that was taught to him. Let that marinate.

There's an invisible war against our lives from the enemy. He wants to distract us and distort the image of our Heavenly Father, so that we never find our identity in God. Satan knows that once we *know who we are in God*, we blow his cover. We will start to see all of his plans, plots, and schemes, and we will be able to hunt down and stop his strategies before he can implement them. He will try to make us hate our natural fathers so that we hate our Father in heaven, because he hates Him. Also, he knows that if we view God with the wrong lens, then we will never understand our purpose in life, and we will never experience the abundant and eternal life on earth, as God has already established in heaven.

Let's not be like the devil. Be willing to let go of your feelings and be free by extending grace and mercy to your loved ones, showing them favor just because, *even when they don't deserve it*. If you don't desire freedom for you and your family, then you will become a prisoner of your own mind, while letting poverty rip the runway in all of your relationships. Why live a mediocre life of constant rejection, fear, abandonment, and lack, when God has called us to a promised life of love, peace, joy, forgiveness, redemption, and freedom? We have to beat the devil at his own game. We have to be better, smarter, and wiser than our enemy.

QUESTIONS FOR REFLECTION

- *Were the adults in your life reliable and responsible? Were promises kept? If not, how did this affect your perception of people in general?*

- *Are you trusting, or do you find yourself doubting people's motives and ability to follow through on what they say?*

- *Would you consider yourself reliable, or do you have trouble following through on commitments? What are some practical ways that you can change this dynamic, starting today?*

CHAPTER 7

THE FAMILY TIE
THAT BINDS

I felt led to discuss this topic as it specifically relates to poverty. Our mindset about how we prosper in life is deeply rooted in our family. God has plans for us not only as individuals, but for the entire family as a whole. What I've learned is that the purpose of each individual family can be revealed by the very thing that keeps a family bound. When you see family members struggling, and they can't seem to shake their addictions, be aware that this is typically what God has called the family to overcome. And we are not just called to overcome our own personal battles, but we are called to pull *other families* out of darkness and into the light of life, deliverance, and freedom.

Have you ever known a family full of teachers, doctors, pastors, lawyers, and businesspeople? Or seen a family where everyone can sing, draw, play an instrument, build houses, or build anything from scratch? These are gifts and talents that God assigns to certain families, and they are not in vain. He plans to use every single gift that He has placed on the inside of us for His Glory and for the advancement of His kingdom. I want to take a minute to take you down memory lane about my family's dynamics so that you can have a clear idea of why poverty is the core of the devil's assignment. The goal of the enemy is to *destroy purpose* in every single family. He wants to keep us from knowing the truth of who we are in Jesus Christ and keep us from the power and authority that Jesus gave us, especially as a family!

WHAT'S IN A NAME?

My family's name is "Alexander," and everyone who knows an Alexander knows *who* and *what* we represent. The name "Alexander" is derived from a Greek word and it means *"defender of the people"* or *"defending men."* Also, *"protector of men."* Names have significant meanings, and they can help to decode our purpose in life. This is why it is so important to not just give your child any old name because you are literally speaking into their life. Furthermore, our names carry weight, and it is exactly where the devil shoots his shot.

The Alexanders, as I have grown to know, are individuals that will go above and beyond to fight battles and protect others. We have a heart of gold, serve others, are funny and uplifting, and we have personalities that people love. We are nurturers, and we meet no strangers—we have the gift of gab! We will talk your ears off if you let us. In addition, we will treat you as our own family, even if you are only dating one of our family members. The energy in our family makes others wish that their family was like ours. I am not saying this to be boastful or prideful, for I've heard this statement on numerous occasions, *"I wish my family was as close as yours."* I didn't realize that other families were not like ours. I mean, we all have our moments where we get mad or offended and stop talking for a while, but we always come back to a place of love. In addition, my family is prophetic; we hear from the Lord, loud and clear. We have visions and dreams. We are gifted with discernment. We are talented and creative with our hands, and we are evangelistic in nature. Some of our talents include the ability to sew, crochet, and knit beautiful blankets and baby clothes, drawing, rapping, poetry, building and reconstructing items from scratch, styling hair, and writing. We are full of engineers, accountants, nurses and nurse practitioners, musicians, singers, pastors, evangelists, and business owners.

Unfortunately, not every member of the family has tapped into their own gifts nor realized how to utilize their gifts to get them out of poverty and change the world. All families have a dark side to them—no one is exempt. There are areas of our lives that are currently hindering us from living the best version of ourselves; a life of total deliverance and freedom of sin and death. Some of areas of hindrance include gossip, lying, deception, drama, bitterness, anger, unforgiveness, and addictions to vices such as sex, money, food, cursing, self-absorbency, pride, fear, jealousy, and perfectionism.

I want to encourage you to do an assessment of your family and allow God to highlight the whys? *Why* is the devil working so hard to keep our family bound? *Why* are we still stuck in all of these issues? *Why* are we divided as a family? The hindrances to our destiny are actually spirits or demons that have entered into our bloodline and have been passed down from generation to generation. And with each new generation, we become tightly tied into a **huge knot** full of sin and death. Our goal should be to break free from the cycles of these generational curses so that we can live a prosperous and abundant life.

THE SINS OF THE FATHER

A lot of what we suffer from in our personal lives has nothing to do with what we are doing, but it may have *everything* to do with our family's past. Past generations have made some decisions, both conscious and unconscious, that we are paying for today. Did you know that the Lord visits the sins of our ancestors even down to the third and fourth generations? The good news of the Gospel of Jesus Christ is that the Lord is merciful to all, and He forgives us of iniquity, transgression, and sin! Praise God!

Exodus 34:7: *"Keeping mercy for thousands, forgiving iniquity and transgressing and sin, and that will be no means clear the guilty; visiting* *the iniquity of the fathers upon the children and upon the children's children unto the third and fourth generation."*

This Scripture lets me know that there are generational curses that have been assigned by hell to keep our families blinded from our true purpose. But glory be to God, we are not responsible for the sins of our ancestors or our parents. **Ezekiel 18:20:** *"The soul that sinneth, it shall die. The son shall not bear the iniquity of the father, neither shall the father bear the iniquity of the son: the righteousness of the righteous shall be upon him, and the wickedness of the wicked shall be upon him."*

While exploring family dysfunction, you cannot simply look at an individual's lifestyle and determine the dysfunction. We must look at how you interact with each family member collectively. If I had to describe my interaction with my family, I would say that my childhood was blessed. My sister and I would spend our summers with our auntie and our cousins, never wanting to leave their house. My sister would hide her shoes so that we wouldn't have to leave; and when my mother came to pick us up, we would beg her to let us stay another night.

During the Christmas season at my cousin's house, there would be Christmas gifts under the tree for me and my sister. I experienced the love of God on our family's life with unity and support for one another. All of us, at some point, lived with one another because someone had fallen on hard times. We stuck together like glue. *Nothing* could separate us, and *nothing* could tear us apart!

If you didn't know any better, you would think that we were all brothers and sisters. I always wanted to be around my family. I have really good memories full of joy and laughter, and I am proud to say that the Lord blessed me with an amazing family. I believe that our connectedness allowed us to share our most vulnerable and our most successful moments in life.

BIRTHING PURPOSE

To dig a little deeper, I want to share with you just how connected I was with my family. In middle school, my cousin, (I'll call him "Mike") came to live with us. He and I shared a room, and we had bunk beds. He was very poetic, always sharing his poetry, and he was funny as all get out. He was a smooth operator. He would share with me stories about the relationships he had with girls, even though I was in middle school and he was in high school. We had developed a trusting relationship with one another, and I felt safe.

I remember when I had difficulty learning a concept in math, he would sit down with me and teach me. He was smart, patient, and creative in his teaching style, which gave me a different way of thinking in order to solve the problem. As a result, math is my favorite subject, and I love to solve problems even outside of math. The relationship with my cousin helped to birth purpose in me. I didn't know it at the time, but his guidance shaped who I was and who I was to become. *His* purpose was connected to *my* purpose and that's why God placed us in the same family.

Mike did not know this; but I looked to him as a positive influence, and I always wanted to make him proud. His teaching approach prepared me to be patient, adhere and yield to wisdom, and it taught me that I could overcome any difficult and confusing situation in life. Growing up, I would subconsciously cover my mouth when I laughed. He would ask me why I covered my mouth and up until that point, I didn't realize that I was doing it. Now, looking back, I know that I covered my mouth because my teeth were jacked! My teeth were so crowded that they looked like they had been playing musical chairs. I was self-conscious about my teeth but wasn't aware that I was ashamed. My cousin's response indirectly gave me affirmation that I didn't have to cover up my flaws, and that I was beautiful regardless of how my teeth looked.

When you have positive affirmations in life, they teach you why you were created. It is the strategic plan of God to staff your life with destiny pushers. Destiny pushers are those who will impart courage in you so that you overcome every obstacle that comes your way! Our families are full of destiny pushers and although our family dynamics may not always be positive, we have pay attention to all of the small lessons because they help to shape our identity.

I can honestly say that my connection and my love for how Mike treated me has caused me to look at him in a positive light. No matter what my cousin is doing, whether it is good or bad, I still view him as a positive influence and an awesome person. Why? Because the Lord has allowed me to see his *heart*. To see what he's *about*. His *purpose* in life. I choose to love the cousin whom God has chosen to be His chosen vessel!

The Lord is faithful to keep families united in love. He will send teachers, friends, coworkers, and family members to show us healthy and functional relationships. Have you ever enjoyed the presence of another person and just wanted to be around them because they were simply amazing? Has anyone ever told you that you were beautiful? That you were smart? That the world needs more people like you because you are a game changer? If not, don't worry. God is aligning you with the right people to set you on the right track. And if the members of your family are not motivating you, then don't be discouraged!

WHO OWNS THE RIGHTS TO YOU?

We all have dysfunctional families, but each member must arrive at a point in their lives where they come to know *who* they are and *whose* they are! Once we allow God to deal with our broken state (poverty) and heal us of our wounds, then we can focus on the bigger picture: family first. What I am saying to you today is that when you choose to be in unity and peace with your family, the devil *does not own the rights to your family.* Just as the saying goes *"I do not own rights to this music,"* the devil does not "own the rights" to us! Jesus purchased us with His blood and redeemed us as His own. He loved us even while we were still sinners (**Galatians 3:13-14** and **Romans 5:8**).

I want to briefly touch on the subject of negative influences, which creates dysfunction. We think and act out behaviors that were taught to us, whether they were verbally taught to us or what we saw in our own eyes. These behaviors trickle down into every part of our lives and I am convinced that they all boil down to one main culprit. That is the spirit of poverty.

As I have discussed throughout my story, there are many spirits connected to poverty. Remember that poverty is a *mindset*. When we see family members doing bad or immoral things, we have a choice. We can choose to follow suit or stay away. Every single person knows the difference between right and wrong. God has imprinted the knowledge of good and evil in our DNA.

Romans 2:14-15 (NIV): *"Even Gentiles who do not have God's written law, show that they know his law when they instinctively obey it, even without having heard it. They demonstrate that God's law is written in their hearts, for their own conscience and thoughts either accuse them or tell them they are doing right."*

It is up to us to make the right decisions by doing the right things and not following the things that would cause us to oppose the will of God.

CONTROLLING THE VOLUME

Every person has picked up habits that are not beneficial for them and that have become strongholds for the entire family. It was through my family's generational curses that I learned how to control and manipulate people with my witty words. I believe having wit and being quick with words can be a good thing, but you have to use it in the right context. For example, I had a friend who was very passive; and whenever we would get into a disagreement or argument, I would talk all over her. I knew that I could get my thoughts and words out faster than she could; and since I felt that I wasn't being heard, I would go overboard and drown her out in order to get my point across. This led to a friendship with poor and ineffective communication, leaving her helpless and unheard, while I on the other hand had a sense of pride about how I was able to handle myself.

I learned this dysfunctional behavior from my mother, cousins, aunts, and uncles. This behavior was a pattern that I first saw manifested in my family. I also saw this occur in how my cousins, aunts, and uncles interacted with their siblings. I observed raised voices and heated arguments when someone felt that they were not being heard or understood. I remember conversations with my mother or sister where they would literally take over the conversation, pushing their opinions and advice, when all I wanted to do was to vent.

Talking over a conversation or raising your voice to talk is dysfunctional all day, every day. It paralyzes and silences one party because the other party has controlled the volume. *Isn't it funny how we treat people the way we don't want to be treated?* We are blinded by our own dysfunctional patterns and don't realize that we are doing the exact same thing that was done to us! Hurting people hurt people!

POVERTY, PIMPS, AND PLAYERS

Another thing I learned was how to do was to be a pimp and a player. Yes, I said it! And if you know me, you're probably thinking, *"No, not Stefani. Not the church girl."* Now, I've never physically pimped a person, but I did pick up some ungodly behaviors that manifested through the generational curse called "lust." Lust typically means *"a strong sexual desire for something or someone, whorish."* However, its roots are manifested in a controlling and manipulative spirit.

Growing up, I got front row seats to seeing this active in the lives of my uncles and male cousins. I saw them spit real game and win women over like it was nothing. Their words were sharp, and their swag was smooth. My cousins and I would always joke, *"Who's our new auntie this week?"* My uncle used to call my sister the "pink pimp" because she "changed her men like she changed her underwear!" Every time we turned around; she had a new boyfriend.

Me, on the other hand? I was witty and smooth with my words and flirting was my middle name. I always joke and say, *"I can talk a man out of his drawers."* As funny as it sounds, it is true. I wasn't the player type, but I could spit game and recognize game. Game recognizes game. I had learned a way of dealing with men.

In my past relationships with men, I often found myself in cycles of sexual sin, only to later find out that I was really looking to fill a void in my life that I didn't know I had. I was filling that void with water instead of filling it with blood—the blood of Jesus. I didn't know that I had "daddy and mommy" issues. I didn't know that I was wounded and looking for my Savior; someone to meet my needs physically and emotionally. I didn't realize that I was lacking the most essential human need, which was love.

LOCKED IN DARKNESS

Between the ages of seventeen and thirty, I was always in a relationship and was never without a man. I settled for mediocre men who couldn't lead me in the right direction because they didn't know the direction that they were headed. The devil kept me locked in their darkness to prevent me from seeing the light. I was broken, wounded, and bleeding on the inside, waiting to be saved and not knowing how to get out. None of the men could affirm, protect, provide, or guide me into the presence of God.

The spirit of lust had me thinking I was in "love" when I was actually in "infatuation." I put their needs before mine because my world revolved around theirs. I lusted after the companionship and relationship that was lacking in my own life with my own family, and I couldn't see that this just wasn't enough.

One day, I woke up and decided that I had had enough. I wanted out of this spirit of lust because it was not getting me anywhere. My future was on hold because I was holding on to someone else's future, not knowing that I could let go at any time. Today, I am proud to say that as a thirty-four-year-old woman, I am free from the spirit of lust and every form of sexual immorality. I thank God that He delivered me from the Jezebel spirit, full of lust and sin! I desired to be free, and the Lord set me free. Even though I no longer operate under that spirit, I still recognize game.

When we talk about recognizing game with the pimp and player mentality, we have to understand the characteristics and actions behind the mentality. Technically, a pimp is *"a man who controls prostitutes and arranges for them, taking part of their earnings in return."* This is the definition that most of us are familiar with, but Merriam-Webster takes it deeper and states that the word pimp, as a transitive verb, is to *"make use of often dishonorably for one's own benefit."* This statement makes it clear that you can also pimp your own family!

I further want to point out that the term "control" means *"an action by which any person who takes over another person's life in return for their own gain."* This means that being controlling is not just limited to a physical aspect, but you can manipulate people with your words by playing on the strings of their emotions. The spirit of lust is the main operating spirit, and it causes an intense enthusiasm for pleasurable delight. So, anything that brings you an intense longing or craving for something can be considered lust. The Bible puts it like this in **1 John 2:15-16**: *"Love not the world, neither the things that are in the world. If any man loves the world, then love of the Father is not in him. For all that is in the world, the lust of the flesh, the lust of the eyes, the pride of life, is not of the father, but is of this world."*

PROTECTING THE GATES

I'm touching on the spirit of lust to show that everything is rooted in something deeper, and it becomes so subtle that we can't initially detect its activity. Many of our families have been struggling with this same issue. The devil knows that if he can get us to fall into sexual sin, then we will be forever craving the pleasures of this world. He sends us on a wild goose chase and keeps us running around in cycles of darkness so that we won't discover our true identity. We must protect our "eye gates," for they are the gateway to our souls. If our eyes are unhealthy, then the whole body is full of darkness, but if our eyes are healthy, then the whole body is full of light (**Matthew 6:22-23**). Our self-serving desires (flesh, eyes, pride of life) block the vision of God, and we cannot see the world or know our purpose from His point of view.

Every person involved plays a pivotal role in the survival of the family. I believe that we are born into certain sins or generational curses that we are meant to break because we are curse breakers. When Jesus died on the cross and defeated death, He rose with all power over the enemy. He redeemed us with His blood as a living sacrifice to set us free from the law of sin and death (**Romans 8:1-3**). And because we are redeemed, we belong to His kingdom and His bloodline!

CHANGING THE STORY

The devil thought he would hang us up to die, but every generational curse that came with our family, Jesus already nailed to the cross (**Colossians 2:14-15**). We don't have to accept what life has dealt us, because we have the power to change the game and overcome *every* obstacle that prevents us from seeing the glory of God. We are no longer bound! The devil can no longer pimp or prostitute our family's giftings for the kingdom of darkness. It is time that we take a stand and show him that we are stronger and better in unity as a family. Let us use our gifts, talents, and words for the advancement of the Kingdom of God, using them for good and not evil. This will ultimately change the trajectory of our family's purpose and set future generations up for life by the sustainable power of God. The Lord said that *"A good man leaveth an inheritance to his children's children: and the wealth of the sinner is laid up for the just"* (**Proverbs 13:22**).

To conclude, the devil does a great job at magnifying the faults, flaws, and ugly sides of us. This is a trick that causes us to disassemble and disconnect from our family. If the enemy can cause chaos, disharmony, and strife, then he can dismantle and destroy an entire generation. Seldom do we reflect on how certain members of our family came through for us during a rough patch in our lives. We become desensitized to our help because our pride has caused us to focus only on ourselves and not others. If all else fails, then at least we have our family.

The devil has perverted the covenant of God's design for family and has used our own destructive behaviors and repeated cycles as a way to keep us all bound. He has blinded us to the point that we cannot see how our life choices influence every single person in the family. If you are reading this book, then it is time to get out of your stinking thinking! If you want to see the chains of poverty broken off in your family line, then I encourage you to take charge. The change starts with *you*, and it takes place in your mind and in your heart. You have to make up your mind that your family has a *purpose*, your family has a *destiny*, and that you are *committed* to breaking the cycle of dysfunction.

QUESTIONS FOR REFLECTION

- *Do you know the origin of your family name? If you had to write a "family creed" what would you say? What does your family stand for? What qualities are you known for?*

- *Is (was) there someone in your family who was an especially positive influence? Have you ever told them how much they mean to you? Write them a letter (even if you do not plan to mail it, or if it is not possible) and tell them how much their investment meant to you.*

CHAPTER 8

CODEPENDENT RELATIONSHIPS

The Holy Spirit gave me insight on how everything that I've talked about in this book so far leads to a very tough topic: codependent relationships. Everything we do in life has some level of dependency. Being dependent means that we put our trust in something or someone as a means for an expected outcome.

WHO DO YOU TRUST?

The very thing that we put our trust into ultimately becomes what we worship…or what takes precedence in our lives. While researching the word "dependence," I found out that it means *"being abnormally tolerant to and dependent on something that is psychologically or physically habit-forming (especially alcohol or narcotic drugs) addiction, habituation, dependence, dependency."* It is also *"the state of being determined influenced or controlled by something else"* (TheFreeDictionary.com).

These two definitions suggest that there is a level of mediocracy and error. It is a dangerous place to put our trust in anything other than the Lord. The Lord warns us about the consequences of not being dependent on Him. In **Romans 1:24-28**, the Word of God says, *"Wherefore God also gave them to uncleanliness through the lusts of their own hearts, to dishonor their own bodies between themselves: who changed the truth of God into a lie and worshipped and severed the creature more than the creator, who is blessed forever. Amen. For this cause, God gave them up unto vile affections for even their women did change the natural use into that which against nature. And likewise also the men, leaving the natural use of the woman, burned in their lust one toward another; men with men working that which is unseemly, and receiving in themselves that recompense of their error which was meet. And even as they did not like to retain God in their knowledge, God gave them over to a reprobate mind, to do those things which are not convenient."*

I want to stop here and discuss what this verse is talking about. These verses pertain to the unnatural affections of women with women and men with men, but the deeper underlying issue is the active pursuit of one's own fleshly desires. God is a god of free will; and if you choose to do something that alters His original design and plan for the nature of mankind, then He will turn you over to a reprobate mind.

What is a reprobate mind? Reprobate means *"morally corrupt or depraved."* One may ask, how can such a loving God do this to His creation? Doesn't He want to provide for, protect, and deliver them? Of course He does, but He is not controlling, and He doesn't have to compete with our idols. He is God Almighty. He is not in competition with anyone. He allows us to make our own choices via our own free will. Also, He has made it very clear in **Exodus 20:3-6** that *"Thou shalt have no other gods before me. Thou shalt not make unto thee any graven image, or any likeness of anything that is in heaven above, or that is in the earth beneath, or that is in the water under the earth. Thou shalt not bow down thyself to them, nor serve them: for I the LORD thy God am a jealous God, visiting the iniquity of the fathers upon the children unto the third and fourth generation of them* *that hate me; And shewing mercy unto thousands of them that love me, and keep my commandments."*

The Lord will allow events to occur in our lives to show us that without complete dependency on Him, we will never be fulfilled or successful at anything in life. Plus, we put ourselves in a bad position with the Lord because our pride prevents us from getting clarity, understanding, and direction from God who holds the keys to our destiny.

HIS PLANS ARE SECURE

The Lord wants us to follow Him and His ways. He said in **Psalm 37:5** that we are to *"commit thy way unto the Lord; trust also in him; and he shall bring it to pass."* This means that God *will not* turn us over to our own idols who can do nothing for us, but He will make sure that the plans He has for our lives are secure. We must completely trust that He knows what He is doing, and we will see Him operate in our lives. Have you ever noticed how children respond to their parents when their parents tell them that they are going to do something for them, such as buy them something or take them to the park? Typically, the child puts their full trust (faith) in that parent while patiently waiting for the end result (the promise). Now, some children get antsy, and they ask a billion questions every day about when it's going to happen, but they still trust that their parents will do exactly what they promised they were going to do.

The childlike faith is one that the Bible teaches us to have in order to enter the Kingdom of God (**Mark 10:15**). Why? Because children are under total dependency on their parents and what their parents possess. We are to depend on the Lord to take care of all of our needs by trusting Him, and by trusting Him we show that we love Him. *"And thou shalt love the LORD thy God with all thine heart, and with all thy soul, and with all thy might"* (**Deuteronomy 6:5**). *"Jesus said unto him, 'Thou shalt love the Lord thy God with all thy heart, and with all thy soul, and with all thy mind'"* (**Matthew 22:37**).

This principle is crucial in the development of our identity and understanding our purpose.

Do you really think that God wants you to struggle your entire life, living paycheck to paycheck, depending on a job or a career to pay your bills, or depending on a man or woman to meet your needs? Let's think about this for a minute. I'm not saying that we shouldn't have a job, career, or significant other. What I am saying is that those things can all be here today, gone tomorrow…and then what?

Our society has taught us to put our confidence in things of the world. It's a system that feeds us a fairytale dream where all you have to do is *"go to school, get a good education, land a good job, make good money, get married, buy a house, have kids, and live happily ever after!"* "Happily ever after!" Yea, that's the part! The "happily ever after" is not so happy after all. No one tells you the dark side of this painted picture of success and happiness. Yes, happiness has a dark side because happiness is dependent on circumstances. One minute, you could be doing well in your career and have great relationships; and the next, you could be upset with someone or have a family death, which causes your whole mood and attitude to change.

We need to know how to navigate through life when all hell breaks loose, and things don't turn out the way that we planned. Furthermore, we need to examine our lives with our eyes open to see what's truly leading our every decision.

Ask yourself now…

- What am I dependent on?

- Am I depending on my job to pay my bills?

- Do I continue in unfruitful relationships because my mama and daddy weren't there for me? Or because I don't like being alone?

- Am I relying on government assistance so that I don't have to work?

- Do I resort to drinking alcohol, smoking cigarettes, or weed to help calm my nerves or to deal with problems in life?

- Do I think I've become successful in life because I worked hard in school and "made it happen?"

All of these questions reveal a dysfunctional one-sided relationship with materialistic and prideful things that keeps us bound and a slave to poverty.

THE SNARES OF THE ENEMY

I believe that the questions above are one-sided because we have become so dependent and blinded by the fact that those things can change once our circumstances change. There is no stability, and it cannot be the only thing we are living with to survive. They can be replaced by *anyone* or *anything* at *any time*. Jesus said that *"man shall not live on bread alone, but by every word that proceedeth out of the mouth of God"* (**Matthew 4:4**).

Harmful substances like weed, drugs, and alcohol are only temporary fixes, and your careers and relationships can be short term. All of these external factors have a negative influence on our lives, and we must pay close attention to the snares of the enemy. We are *"not to be ignorant of Satan's devices"* (**2 Corinthians 2:11**). The devil will use God's good resources as a way to tempt us into putting our trust into everything outside of God.

I was a slave to sin! The mindset of depending on systems and not seeing God as the source of your resource is sin. I lived through the very thing that I am talking about. In 2018, I started realizing that I was born into poverty, and that the ruling spirit over my family was poverty. I was so frustrated with my circumstances that I limited who God called me to be, and I wanted *out*! I recognized that the very thing I was faced with was everything that I was supposed to overcome. I began to feel a burden for the oppressed because I had experienced oppression in every way possible. Two major areas where oppression manifested in my life were my academics and my career.

QUESTIONS FOR REFLECTION

- *What are some things or people in your life that you have been completely dependent on? Is your dependency based on survival, or is your dependency based on filling a void in your life?*

- *Is it difficult to fully put your trust in God if He takes away the people, places, and things that you feel like you can't live without? Why or Why not?*

CHAPTER 9

RETURNING TO THE SOURCE

FINDING OUR COURAGE

I was the first generation of my family to go to college. I attended the University of Illinois at Urbana-Champaign, proudly known as the "U of I Fighting Illini" in 2003. I graduated with my Bachelor of Science in Nursing (BSN) in 2008, then went on to get my Master of Science in Nursing (MSN) in 2012 and became a women's health nurse practitioner (WHNP).

My accomplishments did not come without apprehensions or resistance. I literally had to fight for my sanity and my self-esteem. I was the only Black student in my class of forty-seven students. All of my classmates came from privileged backgrounds, and their parents and family members were nurses, doctors, and pharmacists. I will never forget my first day of class. I spent $900 on books…and I didn't have a clue about nursing. As a matter of fact, no one had ever been sick in my family outside of chickenpox, and no one had ever been hospitalized.

That first day in class, I was praying to God that my instructor would not call on me to answer any questions. I was afraid of not knowing the correct answer, and I was intimidated. Well, the professor called on me; and as my heart raced and beat out of my chest, anxiety took over. I sat there thinking, *"I don't have a clue."* The professor then called on another student. Throughout the week, I remember thinking, *"I don't think I can do this. I don't think nursing is for me."* But I had wanted to help people in the medical field since I was five years old. Somewhere, deep down inside, I found the courage to keep pushing forward and not letting anything stop me.

Another incident occurred during spring break of my last year as an undergrad. I had a mental health instructor whose smile gave you the creeps. I cannot make this stuff up. She would be saying something, then smile, showing her teeth and all for like ten minutes. It was a very awkward and uneasy feeling. Her affect was blunt, with no expression, and she would nitpick things. She once sent a girl home because her sweater was too small, but it actually wasn't. The same girl bought the sweater in a different color but the same size, and the teacher didn't say a thing. The whole experience was crazy; and one day, I had a mental breakdown.

THE SPIRIT OF ANXIETY

I felt like I wasn't going to pass my class, and I believe that the spirit of anxiety worked overtime to cause me to abort the mission that God commissioned me for—to heal the sick. In addition, I wasn't sleeping, I was exhausted, and I was crying all the time. I was so overwhelmed that the teacher must have sensed the stress, because she allowed me to go home for the day. I went to the school's doctor and was prescribed sleeping pills, but I was so stressed that the pills only worked for the first night. I had racing thoughts running through my mind, back and forth, all night long. I later learned that this was a spirit of oppression working with depression. These spirits were designed to push me away from breaking out of generational poverty.

In spite of the intense warfare that I battled, the Lord graced me with the ability to finish strong and to become a registered nurse (RN). After receiving my RN license, I moved forward to becoming a nurse practitioner (NP). I went to NP school part-time, worked as an RN full time, and was a teaching assistant (TA) and clinical instructor for undergrad nursing students. I enjoyed every bit of my transition; however, my excitement changed during one of my WHNP clinical rotations, when I entered into one of the hardest seasons of my life.

I was placed with a certified nurse midwife (CNM) who literally chewed my head off on the first day of clinicals before she even got to know me! For those who don't know, clinicals are a hands-on experience that connects academia to real life training. An MD, NP, or CNM could serve as your preceptor; someone who helps guide, teach, and train you as you learn your new roles as an NP. They serve as a resource and help you to get to a level of competency so that you can master the skills needed when you practice on your own. This was by far the worst and most devastating clinical. Fear gripped me on day one of clinicals, which controlled my thoughts and actions, further diminishing my self-worth and self-esteem.

One day, the preceptor told me that I was just going to observe, but then she put me on the spot. She asked me to explain something to a patient, and I didn't explain it exactly like she wanted it explained, so it made me look stupid. I believe that she did this on purpose because after this incident, she told my course coordinator that she could only take me once a week, when the original plan was for me to be with her twice a week. When I would try to ask her a question for clarity, she would tell me, *"You can just Google that."*

I left clinicals thinking, *"I'm not here to Google anything. I'm here to learn!"* But what this showed me was that she had no interest in teaching me or preparing me for my next level. I was stuck because I needed my hours to graduate, and I was afraid to say a word because I was afraid that it could prevent me from passing that clinical. Once again, I was in a hard place mentally; I lacked the support that I needed to advance myself.

Anxiety struck again, so badly that I would have heart palpitations before I would go to clinicals. My heart would beat so fast that I had to keep taking slow deep breaths to get through the day.

One final incident was the icing on the cake. She asked me a question, and I gave her an answer. She immediately shut me down and in a sharp voice said, *"No. That's incorrect."* I told her that this was what had I learned from my other instructor, and her comeback was *"It's best for you to keep your mouth shut."* My eyes got so big. I could not believe what she had just said to me, and this further indicated that she was on something else. I don't usually pull the "race card," but she was out of line and there was no other reason why she would say this. I know that she didn't like the fact that I was learning something from the other preceptor. The devil tried to use her to keep me from knowing the truth about what I was learning so he could later use it as a weapon to keep me feeling like a failure.

YOU'VE COME TOO FAR TO QUIT

What I want you to see from this part of my nursing journey is that *God called me to this high calling…but the devil wasn't having it.* The anxiety from these situations led me down a road of hopelessness where fear was the driver, and I was tempted to go in a different direction and change careers. I wanted to give up, and I expressed to my mother, my sister, and my godmother that I could just be a travel nurse and make the same amount of money as an NP. They spoke life to me and gave me words of encouragement and told me that I had come too far to quit. They said that if I needed to take a break, take it, but don't throw in the towel. I thank God for my SQUAD! I had to *push through* no matter what. The reason for the push was because there were people out there, waiting for me to cross the finish line so that they could cross over! The health and lifeline of those patients that I took care of in the hospital, and the future of the students that I taught were directly connected to my "yes" to God. Their lives were *literally* dependent on me finishing strong. I had to be totally dependent on God for strength and courage because He wanted to use my life as a conduit of His love and grace. The Lord knew that I would teach people the right and healthy way of living, to be a light in darkness, and that I would heal people in medicine and with my words.

THE PLACES YOU'LL GO

If you are in a situation where your career aspirations are on the line and you have been knocked down by professors, teachers, or even employers, consider yourself safe. God's plan for your life is *so much bigger* than your circumstances. The people you'll meet and the places that you will go will be worth the push. Don't give up in the dark places, because the light always shines in darkness (**John 1:5**). If the devil kills you, then he can wipe out a whole generation; but if you destroy his works, then you have overthrown his kingdom.

The spirit of poverty will fight you on all levels to destroy your destiny and prevent you from entering into a land flowing with milk and honey. After I went through that season of oppression, God placed me with awesome preceptors, who encouraged me and treated me as their own. One preceptor told me that if I felt anxious at any time to let them know, because you can't learn if you're anxious. This was such a relief, and I finished and became a board-certified WHNP. As you know, the devil was big mad, and he was determined to cause me to quit.

When I started my career as a WHNP, I found myself to always be the only Black, the only Christian, and the only one to actually care about the welfare of the women I served. I got into ugly situations where I was treated poorly as a provider. I was lied about, written up, disregarded, and disrespected. I started my journey in 2012, and it is now 2020. I've had good times, and I have had bad times.

I absolutely love what I do, but the devil has been working overtime to kill my purpose in the lives of others. In the past seven years working as a WHNP, I have been laid off four times. Yes, four times! Now, these layoffs were due to restructuring or there just wasn't a need for an NP anymore; however, the crazy thing is, I didn't know that there was such a thing as an NP getting laid off. In addition, I attended a networking workshop where I met an MD and a medical CEO who had also been laid off. This blew my mind, and it taught me that no one is exempt from the hands of poverty.

From the moment I experienced multiple layoffs, I started to wake up, and I found great insight to this whole thing we call *life*. The Lord *has to* be your source in *everything*! Period! I trusted in the Lord, and I believed God for all of His blessings, but He still allowed events to happen in my life which shaped my identity and my dependability on Him. I didn't know this at the time, but God spoke to me about my situation via His prophet. He told me that, *"There was a spirit of poverty over my family that was there to keep us complacent. We would want for nothing but still needed things."* This prophetic word explained the very thing that I was battling, I just couldn't put my hand on it. And although this was reassuring, I still had to do something about it.

A NEW TREASURE

I've discovered a new treasure, the treasure that the Lord wanted to deliver me from the spirit of poverty by delivering me from the dependency of my career. I was used to a bi-weekly paycheck, and when it was taken away from me I was overcome with fear. I was afraid of how I would pay my bills without having that constant flow of income, and I had extreme anxiety about what my financial security would look like in the future. I didn't realize that the *"stability"* from the source of my income was *not* in my *career*...it was in the LORD! Now, don't get me wrong; we need money to pay our bills and to take care of our personal needs, but we have to know that God wants to get the glory out of our lives. Our lives are not our own, because Jesus has already paid the price for them (**1 Corinthians 6:19-20**). I believe that God wants our lives to be a testament of His riches and power, to reassure us that HE IS ABLE and that HE IS THE SOURCE OF LIFE. The hardships we face make us mature and complete in our faith (**James 1:2-4**). Our jobs are our assignments, and the Lord can shut it down at any moment. We must not become comfortable with our situations, careers, or relationships. Our total dependence has to be on the Father.

How do we get to a level of total dependency on God? The answer is simple…yet it is a difficult concept. You have to allow everything to be stripped from you! Total dependence is having faith in God, knowing that *"He shall supply all of your needs according to his riches in Glory in Christ Jesus"* (**Philippians 4:19**). And He is able *"to make all grace abound towards you; that ye always having sufficiency in all things, may about to every good work"* (**2 Corinthians 9:8**). If we seek God's kingdom first and His righteousness, then we will have more than enough added to our lives for our survival (**Matthew 6:25-33**).

Total dependence doesn't mean that you are perfect or that you won't doubt how God will help you in a situation or help you out of a situation. The temptations of life will come not from God (**James 1:13**) but from the enemy. The enemy can tempt us to make poor decisions when circumstances arise, and our faith is shaken. We can either choose to trust in our own way and fall into the trap, or we can trust in the Lord who provides a way of escape (**1 Corinthians 10:13**). There is nothing new under the sun, and the devil uses the same tricks. You have to be aware of your surroundings and circumstances as the devil is always lurking around, seeing who he can devour (**1 Peter 5:8**).

QUESTIONS FOR REFLECTION

- *Can you think of a time in your life where a teacher, a manager, or someone else discouraged you from pursuing your dreams? If so, how did this make you feel? Did you completely give up, or did you find the courage to continue pursuing your dreams?*

- *Are there areas in your life that you have not completely surrendered to God such as your career? What would be the benefits of surrendering those areas to Him?*

- *Have you ever been laid off from a job? What about more than once? If so, did this cause you to see your job as your source of provision, or did it cause you to see God as your provision?*

CHAPTER 10

FINANCIAL REALIGNMENT: WHEN THE LAYOFF PAYS OFF

THE CREDIT TRAP

The Lord is faithful in always giving us an outlet from destructive cycles in our dysfunctional codependent relationships. Outside of one's career, another pathway the devil uses as a destructive trap is the use of credit. I had an addiction to the use of my credit cards. I don't mean addiction as in I had to use my card every single day and for everything, but the behavior was addictive in nature.

The credit card cycle began in my freshman year of college where you could get a free T-shirt and a large pizza if you signed up for a credit card. Well, what college student do you know that doesn't like free stuff, especially food? Plus, everyone else was signing up for a card no harm done, right? I was fortunate that my mother taught me to never spend more than 50% of my credit limit and to always pay my bills on time, which meant to pay them at least one to two weeks before the due date and to only charge the card if I had the money to pay it back, so that I wouldn't be stuck trying to pay a bill that I couldn't afford. The wisdom that I received from my mother helped me to build excellent credit, and I was able to get things I needed at that time. However, I had a problem. My credit card usage was not only being used for things I *needed*, but it was also became used for the things I *wanted*.

I was used to the "swipe and buy" method where you just swipe, swipe, and swipe some more without thinking twice about the cost. It became a form of self-gratification, because I could get anything I wanted since it was at my fingertips. Plus, I didn't have to see my checking account dwindle down to nothing.

I mainly used my credit card for necessities like new tires, a car battery, food, etc. Eventually, I started going over the 50% rule, and I ultimately applied for more credit cards. The credit card industry is a "setup." Establishing credit is a great way to prepare one for purchasing big investments such as a house or a new car; but establishing credit can also lure you into the trap of mindless spending (poverty). I'm no expert on credit card use, but I do know that credit cards with reward or perk systems, such as cash back, can send you into a deep hole of use and misuse.

What do I mean by use and misuse? Well, you can use your card to purchase one item; and the next thing you know, you're using it to purchase other items that you may not need. And before you know it, you become used to using it for everything until your usage is up to about 90 to 95% of the limit. Furthermore, you may pay it off completely, but only to fall into the same cycle of running it up again. We subconsciously use this method of use and misuse, and we fall into cycles of revolving debt. We neither win nor gain; we lose! We lose because our emotions become attached and intertwined with the credit card which hinders us from relying on the true supply and demand—Jesus.

It was during the darkest times of my life that I used my credit cards the most. Those dark times came about when I was laid off of work, and the unemployment benefits were only enough to pay my bills. I would use the credit cards for food and gas for my car, only driving where I absolutely had to go, and I chose cheaper food options that were going to last me a long time.

I remember one credit card was so high, that when I actually looked at my bill, I saw that I was paying more on the interest of that credit card than I was paying on the item itself. It was like buying a pair of shoes for $50 but after paying all of the interest, that same pair of shoes cost me about $150. This baffled me, and I was devastated because I could have just paid for the item in full instead of paying triple the amount. Crazy, right?

IMPULSE SHOPPING

The other wake-up call that I discovered about myself that I want you to be aware of is "impulse shopping." Impulse shopping is a form of addiction where you feel like you've got to get something quickly before the offer is off the table or the fact that you may never see that item again, so you better purchase it now. It's all a trap! It's a mind trap!

One time, I paid off a credit card that I had had for years. The limit was about $4,000, and I was happy to be free of that debt. But during that same year, I purchased a house, and I wanted to do some upgrades. One day, I went to a restaurant and I saw a sign that said, "Eddie Z's Blinds." I was curious, so I walked in and saw some nice blinds. The next thing I knew, I had set up an appointment for a consultation…and guess what? They were having a sale, and I ended up purchasing new blinds for my home that exact same day.

Those blinds were custom-made and cost me about $1,800 for four blinds. I was credit card free, but I fell into the cycle again, and charged my card, thinking I would pay it off within a year, before the interest kicked in. I thought that because I had a low monthly payment for the next year that I was good. This is how they get you, because you don't know the financial state you'll be in in the next year!

When I visited The Container Store for the first time, I was in awe of everything that they had. For those who don't know me, organization and decluttering is my *thing*! I was like a kid in the candy store with an unlimited budget. I spent two hours looking around the store, and I thought I was in heaven. And if that wasn't enough, I saw they had a section specifically for customized closets. I had just said to myself that I wanted to upgrade either my bathroom or my closet in the master bedroom. Things were just too overcrowded, and I needed space to reorganize and declutter.

On that day, I had a good reason to upgrade, because they were having a sale. So, here I was once again, purchasing a new closet on my "spur of the moment" impulse shopping, falling into the trap. Now, to top it off, I got approved for the store's credit card limit of about $3,500, with no interest for twenty-four to thirty-six months. At this time, you couldn't tell me that this wasn't a good decision. I was getting a good bang for my buck.

I had a plan to pay off this debt within one year, before the interest kicked in. I was expecting a bonus from my job, and I eventually got the bonus, but since I had been living paycheck to paycheck, I decided to use that bonus to pay off other bills; hence, I had a little change left in my pocket. So, the credit card remained, and it took me about a year to pay that charge off.

I want to highlight some very important points that occurred between the transactions that I discussed. First, I got out of debt only to find myself right back in the same cycle. And second, it was my connection to the stores that caught my attention. I was caught off guard by the fancy décor and the good deals going on at that time. My intentions were to pay off those credit card balances before the interest kicked in and to pay them in full.

As a result of these debt cycles, I noticed another cycle appeared when I would try to get out of debt; the cycles of back to back layoffs. Poverty struck me over and over again. Every time I came up with a plan to aggressively pay off a huge amount of debt over a short period of time, I would get laid off. The trick of the enemy was to keep me wanting stuff and making me believe that I deserved it because I was financially free. He likes to put his two cents into the equation, but just because you are financially free, doesn't mean you should spend your money any kind of way.

You still have to have good discipline and be a good steward of your money. The overall goal of how the devil uses credit is to keep you thinking that low monthly payment is affordable, and you pay on it as long as you like. We think we are getting a great deal, but it only ends up kicking us in the butt in the long run.

PAYDAY LOANS AND PAWN SHOPS

Another example of poverty that is clear and evident in our society is the use of payday loans. I have seen advertisements, heard about it on the radio and I even know some people who use them. I've never taken out a payday loan, but I know that this system is ridiculously dangerous. It reminds me of when you charge a credit card to a high amount and then you are charged with a high interest rate on top of the balance. You have to pay back more than what you charged. If you take out a payday loan for $100, then you may have to pay back $140. And if you don't pay it back in a timely fashion, then you can expect to have the police knocking at your door.

I heard about a single mother of four who took out a loan for about $4,000 because she was struggling, and I believe that she would have to pay back $5,000 or more. I can only imagine how hard that would be, because she couldn't even afford the $4,000, let alone paying way more than she could afford.

There is one last story I have to mention because I learned something new recently. I found out that you can pawn an item at the pawn shop. They will hold it for you, give you cash, and when you're ready, you can buy it back. The problem with this method is that you have to buy it back for more than what you "sold" it for. I have never used a pawn shop, and I never knew that you could actually get your items back. But isn't this the whole objective of the enemy's plan? To pay a high price.

When we allow ourselves to become a part of a systematic institutionalization of poverty, we become slaves to that system. The Bible tells us that *"The rich ruleth over the poor and the borrower is servant to the lender"* (**Proverbs 22:7**). It was never God's intent that we become slaves to debt, because we are called to be lenders and not borrowers. He gives us power to get wealth, and you cannot gain wealth by remaining in debt(-**Deuteronomy 28:12** and **Deuteronomy 8:18**).

The Lord is the creator of everything, and He gives His creation (humans) His creativity. He will give you ideas to generate wealth with your gifts because your gifts will make room from you (**Proverbs 18:6**). On my journey to financial freedom, I found many patterns and spending habits that prevented me from seeing the bigger picture, which was *"to owe no man nothing but to love him"* (**Romans 13:8**).

It wasn't until 2018 that I decided that enough was enough. The devil had plotted against my destiny by sending forth his weapons of multiple layoffs before I had the chance to actually pay the debts off. It was as if he saw my goals and knew that when I got free, then I would set others free! But I gave the devil a taste of his own medicine. I submitted myself to the Lord, and I told Him that I hated financial poverty just as much as I hate seeing people being lost in their souls. The devil thought he had me in his corner, but I had Jesus as my coach.

FROM FEAR TO FAITH

All those years of layoffs produced a fear in me which caused me to RUN! I ran from fear to faith! The fear of poverty chased me... *but it chased me right into the hands of the Father.* I feared the Lord and knew that He would save and deliver me. The fear of the Lord is not to be afraid (as in being fearful) but fear in Hebrew means *"having reverence for God."* **Proverbs 14:27** states that *"The fear of the Lord is the fountain of Life, to depart from the snares of death"* and **Proverbs 9:10** says that *"The fear of the Lord is the beginning of wisdom: and the knowledge of the holy is understanding."*

I literally wanted nothing to do with evil or lack, and I sought the Lord's wisdom for my financial breakthrough and freedom. When I thought about all of the debt that I had accumulated, it made me sick to my stomach. During those times of unemployment, I often imagined how much money I could save if I didn't have that extra baggage of debt on board. I was so afraid of being laid off again, struggling to pay minimum balances and having money to buy food that I made up in my mind that I was going to GET OUT OF DEBT BY ALL MEANS NECESSARY.

In 2016, I was on my third layoff, and I was going on ten months of not working. I was crushed, oppressed, depressed, and afraid that I was going to lose my home. I could not see my way out of the dark space that had clouded my mind. I was literally losing my mind with no one that could help me figure things out. I recall many days of crying and praying, praying and crying, and intense feelings of doubt, fear and failure flooded my world.

FAITH IN THE FIRE

Throughout all of this mess, I still had some hope deep down inside. I got up every day holding on to the little hope I had, and I would spend hours looking for jobs as a WHNP. The job search is significant because the market for WHNPs is highly saturated yet limited in Illinois, and these positions are not typically advertised or found with online search engines. As you can imagine, I became burned out; however, the Lord gave me a new idea. He led me to research women's health clinics in my area and surrounding areas, print off multiple copies of my resume and references, and drop them off at those clinics.

I got up early one morning, got dressed as if I was going to have an interview, and passed out resumes to those clinics even if they were not hiring. This was a true act of faith. The Bible tells us that *"faith without works is dead,"* and that we should *"be still and know that He is God"* (**James 2:14-20** and **Psalm 46:10**). Nothing ever came about my job search even after following up on my resume release, but I did something rather than nothing. I was exercising my faith in God by being *still* which was resting in His promises (His Word, the Scriptures) that He would provide for me. The devil wants to kill our faith because he knows that it pleases God.. *"Without faith it is impossible to please God"* (**Hebrews 11:6**).

In my journey to financial freedom, I thought my career as an NP was over. I worked so hard to get to where I was and to just throw everything away was like building a house only to have it be swept away by a tornado the next day. I can remember family and friends saying to me, *"Why don't you just go back to being an RN at the hospital?"* and *"You might need to file bankruptcy, so your house won't go into foreclosure.*" But I had a different viewpoint, the inside scoop on my situation, and these suggestions were not how we do in the Kingdom of God. The Lord wants us to put our full trust in Him. Don't get me wrong, it is wise to listen to and heed to advice provided by those around us, but we need to weigh what we hear by the wisdom of God. I gave those "extra" ideas to the Lord to see if I needed to reconsider how I viewed my current situation. As I waited for the answer, my faith was truly tested in the fire. The unemployment benefits were running out, and fear wrapped itself around me and tried to squeeze the life out of me. The heat was turned up, and I was overwhelmed by what would happened next when I ran out of money with no income coming in. By this time, I came to a new place of surrender. The faith and hope that was inside of me helped me to realize even though I was at the end of the road that the Lord promised to meet me at the crossroads, and He would supply ALL of my needs (**Philippians 4:9**).

MY NEEDS...GOD'S WANTS

The ultimate faith finder is when you have fully surrendered your will over to the Lord. I was at the end of my rope, and I said to God, "*Okay God. You can have my job and my career. If you want me to go back to being an RN at the hospital, then I'll do just that. Send me where you need me to be, not where I think I should go.*" The above prayer was super powerful and dangerous, because *I no longer put my needs before God's wants.* I did away with pride and demonstrated true humility and reverence for God. After I made this statement, the devil must have heard me because fear tried to put its hands around me once the unemployment officially ran out. But I continued to take a different approach, I trusted God now more than I had been in the last ten months. I said to Him, "*Okay God. I'm putting this in your hands. I can't see how you will provide but I trust you.*" God is faithful, y'all. The Lord put it on my friend's heart to all of a sudden send me funds via Chase Quick Pay as a "just because," and He also put it on my mother's heart to ask me to clean her house, and she would pay me! You see how God makes a way out of no way? He promised and said

"Behold, I will do a new thing; now it shall spring forth; shall ye not know it? I will even make a way in the wilderness, and rivers in the desert (**Isaiah 43:19**). My faith allowed God to move on my behalf. I was able to pay my bills and buy groceries…and then the Lord showered me with His love and His favor, and He did the impossible.

In February of 2017, I was entering my second month with no income and had no idea where my next provision would come from, when I happened to see a job pop up, and I couldn't believe my eyes. It was a WHNP position not too far from my home. I applied and got an immediate response. I had an interview a few days later, and it was everything I was looking for in my new job. By the end of the week, they were down to the last two candidates, and I had a group interview. During the one-on-one portion of the interview, the doctor that owned the practice told me that she felt like I just "fit" there. I told her, *"I do!"*

FREEDOM!

I left the interview with high hopes of receiving it, because I had already declared that this was my job! The next day, I received an email offering me the position as not just an RN but my dream of remaining as a WHNP. Praise Break! Glory be to God. Won't He do it? And to top everything off, my new job was located on Freedom Drive! The Lord showed me that I was finally free. I was free from *fear*. Free in my *thoughts*. Free in my *finances*. Free in my *faith*. Free in my *mind*. Free from *poverty*…and I was *free in Jesus!*

> I want to share with you the riches found in one of the darkest moments in my life. I gave my life to Jesus Christ in order to *live*. I gave up the very thing that I was deeply passionate about in exchange for where HE wanted me to be. My career was everything to me, and I put too much trust in the career instead of trusting in the Lord who gave me the career. I became so dependent on my job to pay the bills that I took my eyes off the One who really pays the bills! His name is Jesus, and He is Lord and Savior of this world. All I had to do was to submit to His way and surrender my plans for His plans.

Poverty can cause us to hold on to things that have the ability to shape our identities. We become attached to the very things that are conditional and subject to change, fail, and disappear. You can have a job today, and it can be gone tomorrow! I believe the Lord allowed these events to happen to me to show me just how great His love is for me and to upgrade my faith. The Lord wants all of us to put our trust in Him and to know that He is the Source behind the Resource!

I can say that 2017 was a great restart in my pursuit of both financial freedom and freedom from codependent relationships with my credit card and my career. In trusting God in the process, I have to add the other miraculous things God did for me in my time of transition. I applied for a program that helped to provide financial assistance to those who had a drop in their income and had difficulty paying their mortgage, called the Illinois Hardest Hit Fund (HHF). This fund will either pay the amount of mortgage payments that you missed, or they will pay your mortgage payments for up to a year.

I had already used my savings to pay my mortgage for one month. I was five months behind, and this program took about ninety days to get approved. But the Lord gave me a miracle; I was blessed with funding to pay the missed mortgage payments *and* my mortgage was paid for an entire year! Praise God again! Remember when I said that there was an option to file bankruptcy? The Lord said, *"NOT SO."* His will prevailed. He does not let His children fall into the open pits of hell. We have to be open and willing to obey Him and trust Him at His Word. There is a secure plan for your future, for God knows the end from the beginning (**Jeremiah 29:11**, **Isaiah 46:10**, and **Revelation 22:13**).

THE WILDERNESS SEASON

There is a supernatural encounter that happens when adversity strikes. During times of adversity, you enter into a season in your life called the wilderness. Your "wilderness season" is when you are in transition to your next season. The wilderness is a place where you get great clarity on the call of your life, and it tests your faith. My wilderness was being laid off, and it is where I learned to seek the face of the Lord, to stand on His promises and to face fear with courage, knowing that the Lord was fighting for me. My job was a new page turned over in my book. It was a place where I was allowed to be my true self, and I could spend more time with my patients.

With all of the blessings, I started paying off debt as I had planned, and I even inspired a friend of mine to get out of debt. I disciplined myself and did not use any credit cards until they were all paid off. My mindset shifted and was motivated by the thought of never being in this position again.

Let's fast forward to late 2018. The Lord began to burden me with the idea of wanting more out of my life. My new job was enjoyable, but it became a place of "bondage in comfort." I wasn't paid the best nor did I have benefits such as health insurance or paid time off. I felt that it was time to grow in my career and demolish debt for good, so I prayed about it; and a few months later, a door opened to a new position. I had been at that job for eighteen months, and I feared that if I left, that it would be a ticket to round four of the layoffs. This was the fear of poverty.

I also felt guilty for leaving, because this was the only employer that gave me a chance when there was not a job in sight, and I really liked my boss. But I knew that it was time to level up, and I had to step out of my comfort zone, even if I had to do it afraid. I once again gave it to the Father, and I took a huge step of faith.

Have you ever seen the painting where there's a man or a woman walking off a cliff, blindfolded, and there is nothing but water underneath, with a set of hands reaching out to catch them if they fall? This painting was created by an artist named Kevin Williams, and it is a good depiction of what it means to trust God. It is literally called "Step Out on Faith." I was completely trusting God, unable to fully see what lay ahead of me for my future.

I interviewed for the new position and got the job. I had full benefits, including a very generous PTO package and health insurance. And my salary was a $35,000 yearly increase over my last salary. I believe that God saw me steward well in the little amount that I earned, so He rewarded me for my diligence in serving Him (**Hebrews 11:6**).

I started my new position in October of 2018, and I aggressively tackled the remaining debt. I limited my spending on restaurants, and I cut off all unnecessary expenses. I cut the cable off and got rid of the monthly car wash membership and other automatic memberships that I did not need. Then I decided to tackle the credit card with the highest amount of debt first.

In the early part of 2018, I paid off about $13,000 in debt and $2,000 of that included a high-limit credit card. In January of 2019, I had a plan to demolish the remaining $4,000 within two to three months. I started paying $1,000 every two weeks, and by March of 2019, I had completely paid off this credit card. I used my income tax return to pay off a small student loan.

I'm not writing this story to show you how much money I had. I am showing you that the amount of money used to pay down debt could have been used to put in a savings account or buy a new house. There was a shift in my thinking from I could be free to I was already free. I don't want you to think that this was an easy task. There were items that I wanted to buy at the moment and vacations that I wanted to take—but I stayed focused. I had to renew my mind daily and focus on why I was getting out of debt in the first place. I never wanted to be in a situation where I owed someone something, and I had to borrow money to pay off debt, which was still like paying debt to get out of debt. This just didn't make sense; getting out of one jail just to jump into another one.

YOUR FOOD IS EATING YOUR MONEY

Another area that poverty starts to chew away at is your food. We may not think that is a big deal, but your food could be burning a hole in your pocket. Many people say that they don't have enough money to do things, but I beg to differ. I can look at someone's bank account and tell exactly where their money is going. Out of sight, out of mind, right?

I am convinced that most people spend the majority of their money on food, particularly on restaurants. This may not be applicable for everyone, but I believe that we can all agree that we can afford to cut down on our food expenses. You can spend $5 here and there, but it all adds up and before you know it, you've spent $300 a month on fast food.

This was certainly the wake-up call for me; and not only did it put a dent in my checking account, but it added some extra inches to my waistline. I gained such an excessive amount of weight from eating take-out food daily during my lunch breaks that I was unable to fit into any of my clothes.

The mismanagement of our finances can lead to a continuous cycle of lack while causing strain in our mental, emotional, and physical health. I initially lacked the discipline needed to keep my eye on the prize, and my health started to decline as a result. I meal prepped which not only helped me to lose weight and fit my clothes again, but it helped me to save money. If you want to be free, you must get out of your comfort zone, examine your spending habits, and do the work!

There are benefits to completely coming out of your financial jail. Once, I paid off two small student loans and all of my credit cards, and I felt euphoric. It was as if I was in real shackles, and someone unlocked the chains and set me free. The Word says, *"If the son makes you free, you will be free indeed"* (**John 8:36**). Jesus has set us all free! If you have accepted Him as your Lord and Savior and believe God raised Him from the dead (**Romans 10:9**), then He will also raise you from the dead. He will give you access to His debt-free plan in your emotions, your relationships, and your finances.

THE BENEFIT OF THE UNKNOWN

I thank God for His infinite wisdom, and the courage to move me out of my comfort zone and into the place of the unknown. The fear of the unknown keeps a lot of us from stepping out in faith, but the Lord wants us to trust that HE IS THE UNKNOWN and that He is loaded with benefits (**Psalm 68:19-21**). One benefit I enjoyed as I paid off those cards was the excitement I felt when I checked my balance and it was zero. I checked my balance every day because I couldn't believe my own eyes. I was able to see the fruit of my labor, and my sacrifice was not in vain.

Another benefit of being free in the mind is that once your mind is made up, you will not go back to the place of oppression. When I was in grocery or clothing stores, the idea of using a credit card for a purchase would pop in my head but the negative relationship that I had encountered with credit cards persuaded me to think twice about utilizing them. I was more convinced now than ever that I couldn't afford to put myself back into that type of bondage.

I am human, and I would put things on credit from time to time. The goal was to pay it off ASAP and not wait until the billing cycle goes through. I currently have decided that if it is not a necessity, then I don't need to charge it, period! Overall, I believe that credit cards with rewards can be beneficial, but they can also be used as a snare from the enemy. You have to establish a plan for strict discipline and dedication to creating boundaries in your spending as well as your dependency on the Lord.

Getting out of debt is one thing, but staying out of debt is another thing. It all starts in your mind. If you don't discipline your money, then it will discipline you! Don't allow the fear of financial and job securities become your god, but allow God to be God!

QUESTIONS FOR REFLECTION

- *Do you use credit cards? Do you pay them off every month, or carry a balance? Have you ever sat down and looked closely at your spending? Take some time now to do so.*

- *Are there purchases on your credit cards that you would not have made if you had to pay cash? Are there purchases on them that would be considered "normal living expenses" such as food, utilities, etc.?*

CHAPTER 11

PLAN B

By now, I hope that you can see that the spirit of poverty is a real thing. Poverty is Satan's most commonly used weapon which keeps us from the promises and the inheritance of God (His Word of Truth). It would behoove me if I did not discuss a major setback to any form of freedom: Plan B. We can all agree that having a plan is good, but what happens when you have a plan B for the plan B? Sounds a little crazy, right? Well, this has been the story of my life. I was taught to always be prepared for the worst, and to always have a plan.

The Lord has given me the gifts of administration, organization, and planning. People with this give have "Type A" personalities. Everything we do is very detailed-oriented and involves well-thought-out plans that anticipate issues that may arise down the road. It is a mindset that's similar to having an emergency exit plan.

THROUGH THE FIRE

Let's say for example that you develop a plan for your family in case of a fire. If you have front and back doors, and the fire is at the back door, then your goal would be to go out the front door. But what happens if there is a fire at both of the doors, or if one of the doors is jammed? Then the next plan of action may have to be to either run through the fire or to jump out of the window. God forbid this to ever be the case, but you have to have a safety plan in place to anticipate problems that potentially derail the original plan.

Emergency plans are beneficial in emergency situations but can also be detrimental when we use them in everyday, nonemergency situations. I'm talking about Plan B. In order to fully illustrate this concept, I want to break down what it means to be Plan B. First, if you look at the letter "B" in Plan B, we noticed that it comes after the letter A. It is the second letter of the English alphabet. What this means is that the letter "B" was never chosen to be the first letter because there is a systematic approach to the letters in the alphabet. The plan was to make the letter "A" the first letter.

The "B" in Plan B creates a space that allows for and suggests *"an error is likely to occur, and we have to be prepared if Plan A doesn't go through as planned."* It gives one the illusion of a safety net called the *"just in case."* Let's apply this concept to your health. Have you ever heard of the Plan B pill? The Plan B pill is also known as the "morning after pill" and it is used to prevent pregnancy in the event that someone should have unprotected sex. The pill consists of large amounts of the hormone progesterone, which is also found in birth control pills. Progesterone is actually the hormone of pregnancy, creating a safe place for a fertilized egg to grow. But, if given in high amounts, it can prevent a woman from ovulating. Many people think it is an abortion pill; but if a woman has already ovulated, then it will not have any effect on the unborn baby. The goal is to prevent an unplanned or unwanted life. In the same way Plan B works, is the same way most of us live our lives.

The purpose of Plan B is to ultimately stop the plans of God. We can all attest to the fact that at some point in our lives, we've had a Plan B. Most times, our back-up plan is created out of fear! The fear of Plan A not working, or the fear of what we perceive as fear, could be a potential threat to what we are trying to accomplish. This purpose of using the Plan

B pill is to prevent a woman from having an unwanted pregnancy. She has been taught that a pregnancy is likely to occur if no condom is used or the condom breaks. This perception is a true reality, but the decision to engage or not to engage in sex is rooted in fear.

THE FEAR OF THE UNKNOWN

Anytime you see a level of stagnation in your life, you can expect to find the spirit of fear behind your back-up plan (Plan B). Fear runs deep into our family roots and was seen with Adam and Eve. When the serpent tempted Eve with the idea that she would not surely die if she ate from the Tree of Life, she was lured in by the enticement of her own fear (**Genesis 3:2-4**). She feared the unknown and the thought that maybe God was not God and that He was holding something back. It caused Eve to doubt God (Plan A) and choose her own route, which was the serpent's plan (Plan B). The decision to choose Plan B when the Lord is Plan A, will cause a separation from the Will of God.

The Lord's Word tells us that, *"There are many devices in a man's heart; nevertheless the counsel of the Lord, that shall stand"* (**Proverbs 19:21**). I love how the Message Bible puts it, *"We humans keep brainstorming options and plans, but God's purpose prevails."* This goes to show that no matter what "your" plan is, God's plan will always be superior, and it takes top priority. The plan of man has a direct correlation and spiritual connection to the battlefield of fear versus faith.

WHAT IF?

Often, we want something tangible…something we can *see* or *feel* in order to validate our next move in life. We are prone to doing what God has called us to do, but only if we can see it with our own eyes and if we know how things will turn out in the end. Only God knows the end from the beginning (**Isaiah 46:10**). Many times, we don't feel secure in our decisions because we are too focused on the "what ifs." *"What if they don't come through? What if I don't get the job? What if I can't pay the bills? What if I'm left with nothing?"* All of these questions are destructive devices that the enemy uses to distract us. He distracts us by planting the seeds of negative comments and lies. He never gives us the full picture. But the Lord shows us our future by stating the opposite of what the devil says. The Lord is saying to you today, *"What if what you fear will never happen? What if you get the job? What if I give everything you need?"* See, the Lord wants us to be free in our minds because this is where our decisions are made.

In addition, we have to be confident in knowing the voice of the Lord and knowing that He has the master plan. You don't need a backup when the Lord leads and guides you to what is true, what is right, and what is HIS WILL. He gives us the things that we should be focusing on, *"Finally, brethren, whatsoever things are true, whatsoever things are honest, whatsoever things are just, whatsoever things are pure, whatsoever things are lovely, whatsoever things are of good report; if there be any virtue, and if there be any praise, think on these things"* (**Philippians 4:8**). And He gives us the perfect antidote against the devil's mind games, *"Thou wilt keep him in perfect peace, whose mind is stayed on thee: because he trusteth in thee."* **Isaiah 26:3** Jesus said that, *"He is the Way, the Truth, and the Life."* **John 14:6** God's Word illuminates every dark pathway, highlights every unknown plan, and makes all things possible (**Psalm 119:105** and **Matthew 19:26**).

The enemy's kryptonite is the Word of God, which is the *light*. He loves to keep us in the dark because he knows that as long as we don't let our light shine, then we'll always be afraid of the dark. It's just like children when they are scared of the dark—they get under the covers and close their eyes. They literally stay in darkness because of the fear that what is outside of the covers is scarier than being underneath them. The "covers" represent our Plan B...our comfort zone because of what we *think* is on the other side.

STEPPING OUT OF OUR COMFORT ZONE

The fear of stepping out of our comfort zone causes stagnation in the journey to our destiny. Fear paralyzes you, and it is a destiny destroyer. Fear will prevent you from pursuing your dreams and fulfilling the calling that's on your life. It also causes you to disobey God and prevents you from making vital decisions that could set you up for life. Fear gripped me in the place of employment.

As I mentioned earlier, the Lord allowed me to get a new job and to pay off a massive amount of debt. The new place of leaving a job was out of my comfort zone because I was used to getting laid off. I knew that I had to make the decision to leave; and that if things didn't work out, then I would be responsible for unemployment. I had the fear of poverty striking yet once again in my life. However, this is not how the Lord saw it.

Approximately six months after I started the new job, in April of 2019, I was in a car accident and badly injured my left wrist. I literally shattered all of the bones in my wrist. This situation put me in a place of true humility. I couldn't use my left hand at all. I couldn't drive, cook, or clean so I had to have cleaning services and meal delivery services. I had severe swelling, pain, numbness, and tingling in my hand and fingers. And to top it off, my new job terminated my position since I was unable to return to work on their terms. I was not surprised, but God had been preparing me for this fourth layoff, especially since I had been through it so many times.

Despite what happened to me, the Lord showed me that I was actually blessed, and I was rewarded for my obedience to Him. I left my previous job in fear of losing a new job, but I was able to walk in full confidence and victory. I know that the Lord led me to the new place of employment, and He led me out of debt. The blessing and the reward were that I now had health benefits that could be the cushion for the financial hit that I took from hospital bills. Can you imagine if I had stayed at my old job with no health benefits and gotten into the car accident? And can you imagine how I would be treated without medical insurance?

I work in healthcare, and I've seen both sides of the spectrum. Those who do not have health insurance are less likely to get the proper diagnostic testing needed to fully assess the severity of their illness or injury. I always thank God for His protection, but I am most thankful that I made a decision to upgrade my life. I stepped out of my comfort zone at the right time.

Even though I was only on my new job for six months, I was able to get completely out of debt, and it allowed me to see the light at the end of the tunnel. Also, the time that I have been off work recovering has allowed me to heal not just physically but also emotionally from all the past mother, father, and family wounds. I've had time to process my life and my desires, and I've learned to love and take care of myself. The Lord allowed this event to happen to me to slow me down and to give me time to write this book you are reading today!

NO LONGER A SLAVE

The devil thought he could stop the plans of God from operating in my life. He tried to attack me by breaking my wrist in an effort to prevent me from testifying about how God delivered me from the spirit of poverty— but he was dead wrong. He thought I would follow him in fear and with the guidance of my emotions, but I decided to follow the Lord. **John 10:5, 27** (paraphrased): *"The Lord has established in His word, that his sheep know His voice and a stranger he will not follow."* I thank God for allowing His plans to prevail. I made a decision, and I chose to get out of fear, which had become my comfort.

*I am no longer a slave to **poverty**... because I am no longer a slave to **fear**!*

I truly believe that it is God's desire and ultimate plan that we do not live in lack. Jesus came to the Earth, and He became poor so that we could be rich (**2 Corinthians 9:8**). He also came so that we can have life and have it more abundantly (**John 10:10**). When we talk about being rich or poor, it doesn't just mean monetary or materialistic, but it also means that we have the power and the authority to overthrow the kingdom of darkness. If you've already accepted Jesus as your Lord and Savior, then you have inherited the Kingdom of God. The most beautiful part of the Kingdom of God is that it is not a place that we can find. Actually, the Kingdom of God is within you (**Luke 17:20-21**). You will never need a Plan B with God because He has already promised that we would have everything that we need (**Mark 6:25-33**).

God has a plan for our lives with an expected end (**Jeremiah 29:11**). He gives us the power to get wealth (**Deuteronomy 8:18**), and He gives us the power and courage to do His will (**Philippians 2:13**). Having your own Plan B only delays the progression of your life, which can alter the divine connections of people, places, and things that you are supposed to encounter.

Do not miss the opportunity to advance yourself in life because of fear. Fear grips poverty, and poverty grips fear. They are both romantically in love with one another, working overtime to keep you from loving yourself. You have to LIVE LIFE in the moment and embrace everything it has to offer.

The Lord wants all of us to be free. He paid the highest price (**Galatians 3:13-15**), and He redeemed us from the law of sin and death (**Ephesians 1:17**). He calls us His own, and He calls us by our name. We belong to Him (**Isaiah 43:1**). God's will for our lives is found in our identity in Him. His Word is His promise. Jesus is the promise, and Jesus is the written Word (**Revelation 19:13**). The Lord Jesus has already cancelled every debt, every decision, and everything that has kept us in slavery. He cancelled it by nailing it to the cross that He was hung from. It no longer belongs to us. We can be 100% assured that Jesus already disarmed the principalities and the powers of darkness that were against us (**Colossians 2:14-14**).

We no longer have to *live* like slaves, *act* like slaves, or *behave* like slaves. It is time to take our power and our authority and declare out of our mouths that we are no longer going to allow fear to strip us of our right to be rich in Christ Jesus. The fear of poverty can only have access if we give it access, but we learn to disarm it by the WORD OF GOD.

No longer shall we let the devil get away with stealing our joy, our peace, our emotions, our plans, our finances, our relationships, our family, our future, nor our faith. I charge you today to find the light within you, and allow your light to shine!

DO YOU WANT TO BE FREE?

The Lord has a plan, a purpose, and a destiny for your life. He doesn't want you to live a life without purpose or direction. Nor does He want you to remain in lack, fear, or hopelessness. He wants you to experience an overflow of His *direction*, His *peace*, His *freedom*, His *hope,* and His *love*!

From my journey, you can see that my relationship with the Lord Jesus is the foundation of my perseverance. And just as He has brought me out of poverty and into prosperity, He wants to do the same for you!

My question for you is, *"Do you want to get to know the Jesus that I know?"*

If you do not know the Lord Jesus or you have never accepted Him into your life and you want to become a part of His family, I invite you today to receive Him as your personal Lord and Savior! It is very easy to accept Him. I will guide you through a prayer of faith that will help you begin your new journey of life! Say this prayer out loud:

Dear Lord Jesus,

I know that I am a sinner, unworthy of your love, but I repent for all of my sins, both known and unknown. I can no longer live a life in darkness...and I need you. I confess with my mouth that you are Lord; and I believe in my heart that you died on the cross for my sins, and God raised you from the dead with all power. You have washed me white as snow in your blood, and you have redeemed me as your own! Thank you for forgiving me of my sins. I receive you into my heart as my personal Lord and Savior to live an abundant and eternal life in you! Amen.

CHAPTER 12

FINALLY FREE:
THE SETBACK WAS A SETUP

The spirit of poverty is *truly* a mentality. It conditions the brain to default to Plan B without exploring God's initial plan. As you can see, the devil's primary mission is to destroy God's kingdom. He wants us to be ignorant of his plans, plots, schemes, and devices. If he can keep us tied up in our minds, then he can change our attitudes and behaviors in life. Our attitudes and behaviors determine our success in life.

THE MEASURE OF SUCCESS

Success looks different for different people. Some measure success by their accomplishments. Some measure by the number of materialistic things that they acquire. For me, the measure of true success is overcoming poverty and taking a stance against the kingdom of darkness. From my testimony, you can see that poverty invests itself into our lives when we are children, partnering with our growth and development, and it gains interest on our thoughts, habits, and behaviors. The devil is only interested in his return. He sows the seed by feeding us his lies; then he waters it by increasing the intensity of our circumstances, and we take the bait by getting entrapped in a whirlwind of sinful living.

Poverty is a sin that brings forth death of our destinies because it separates us from having a relationship with the Father. **James 1:15** says, *"Then when lust hath conceived, it bringeth forth sin: and sin, when it is finished, bringeth forth death."* We have to be very careful to not allow our desires to forfeit our freedom, which is our life.

God not only wants us to *get* free, but He desires that we *remain* free. This book was created to show you how there are so many spirits working and linking together with poverty in order to keep you in chaos and confusion. If you closely examine your life, you should be able to see poverty in all areas of your life. Our lack of understanding of who we are in God shows us that there is a lack, a need, or a void present in our life. Because of this void, we began to think and act like an orphan, doing everything we can to gain the acceptance and the approval of others. We work harder, we struggle more, and we become slaves to our desires.

LOW-LEVEL LIVING

It is also difficult to make wise decisions because we get trapped into the same cycles year after year. When will you decide that enough is enough and that you are ready to live? When will you decide that you want to be free from emotional instability and painful experiences? When is it time for you to level up and stop living on the "Triple L?" The "Triple L" is LOW-LEVEL-LIVING. In order to get ahead in life and come out on top, you must change your thinking about who you *are* and who you were *created to be.*

> If you want to see change, you have to be changed!

Yes, many of us were born into poverty, but it doesn't mean that we have to *stay* in poverty. You have the power to break free from any and everything that was passed down through your family's bloodline. You have the right NOT TO ACCEPT the hand that was dealt to you.

We are called by God to be the change agents for our families and our friends. It all starts in our mind. We must DECIDE that there has to be a new norm, a new way of living that brings joy and peace. The decision to change the game is crucial not just for ourselves, but also for generations to come. The Word of God tells us that *"a good man leaves an inheritance to his children's children and that the wealth is laid up for the just"* (**Proverbs 13:22**).

What are you laying up for the future generations? What the legacy will you leave for your family? What strategies have you instilled in your family that will cause them to live off the wealth of the wicked? Think about such things. The Lord is so amazing because He gives us everything we need to live a godly lifestyle. Godly doesn't mean "holier than thou." It means a life full of the goodness of God. It is a life full of joy, peace, surety, stability, provision, and direction.

It is certainly NOT God's will that we live a life of confusion, hold grudges against one another, live paycheck to paycheck, or be drowning in debt. Furthermore, He wants us to be free from fear; fear of the *unknown*, fear of *failure*, fear of *man*, and fear of *low self-esteem*. Tomorrow is not promised, but TODAY is a day where you can decide that *you've had enough* of mediocre living.

I decided that enough was enough and that I was going to take control of my life once and for all. After being laid off four times within the last seven years, I really began to question my purpose on earth. Was I supposed to be working as a WHNP, only to keep getting laid off? Or was the Lord trying to show me that there is more on the inside of me?

I believe that the Lord was showing me that being a WHNP is only a piece of my purpose, but not my purpose as a whole. He used the setbacks of every traumatic life event to prepare me for my future. Every mother and father wound, sibling rivalry, and relationship and emotional dysfunction was used to shape my character and build my faith. These life lessons have taught me what to do and what not to do, how to respond and how not to respond.

LIVING MY BEST LIFE

I learned that I am strong and courageous, because my Father goes before me and fights for me in all situations. I learned that *all things work together for my good*" (**Romans 8:2**). Furthermore, these obstacles created a new level of strength and birthed a desire in me to want more out of life. I gained confidence in myself, and I gained confidence in the Lord. I can recognize fear a mile away, and I know how to combat poverty with the Word of God. I am no longer terrified of losing a job, because the Lord's history of provision with me is solid.

In addition, my setbacks set me up so that I can *live my best life!* In 2019, I had a complete mindset change. I now have the desire for entrepreneurship, something I had never considered before. The Lord had been telling me that He would bring me out of the corporate world and into entrepreneurship, but this word plagued me. I didn't know what it meant to be an entrepreneur, and I had not seen it done in my family.

I was afraid to walk the waters of uncharted territory, and it was scary to thing about leaving everything I knew (nursing), and moving into a completely different profession where I had not been trained. I was devastated, and I wrestled with this all year. The devil threw his weapon of fear at me once again; but this time, I was prepared. I started thinking that *the only way to get rid of fear is to face fear*! I prayed and asked the Lord for the courage and the strength to take a leap of faith.

The devil had been planting seeds of discouragement, and I felt myself slip into the ugly patterns of poverty. I literally had to speak out loud to myself and tell myself that I could do it and that I would be successful. I used the Scriptures, the Word of God, to combat and neutralize the fiery darts of hell. I had to overcome the heaviness of needing to know how it would all play out. I didn't feel supported, and I doubted how God wanted me to carry out this assignment.

Well, let me tell you, prayer works. The Lord placed good friends in my life to encourage me and to support my business plan. He even sent a friend who specializes in helping entrepreneurs succeed. Furthermore, He used another person to supply me with the items I needed for my business. God set me up. He showed me that I can be very successful and that I don't have to depend on corporate America to do it. God reminded me of what He said, *"What do you have to lose?"* I realize that it's hard to find a job, so I'll just create my own job.

God has given each of us creative abilities to create wealth for ourselves, but we have to believe in ourselves and believe that the vision that God gave us is not in vain. Our business goal is to have the objective of changing people lives by bringing solutions to their problems and to glorify God. I believe that God has given me multiple dreams to help those in need, and I have decided to no longer sit on my gifts and talents. I no longer want to be addicted to "I didn't know how I was going to make it." I'm determined to advance God's kingdom, shining light in darkness and building wealth for my generation and the future generations. Generational wealth is the kind of legacy that I want to leave for my children and my children's children.

I am *not* saying to quit your job because God has given you a dream to become an entrepreneur. What I am saying is to look at all of the possibilities of generating income and to enter into a space where you create your own reality. There is more than one way to skin a cat…and there is more than one way to get out of poverty. We can get out of it by changing our mentality, investigating our relationships, examining our finances, investing in new ventures, and trusting in our Lord Jesus Christ.

I am stepping into new areas that I never knew I could be successful in, and I realized that I don't have to participate in the hustle and bustle demands of working a nine-to-five job. I can work part-time and still own a business. And if I want, I can go full time in business for myself and have multiple streams of income. If there is one thing that I've learned in my life, it would be that I was created for more, more of what I know, and more of what I don't know. I am destined to go higher heights and deeper depths in life. We all are! The awesomeness of the Lord's pour is that He gives you beauty for your ashes (**Isaiah 61:1-3**). Your trials, and tribulations are not in vain, and He will use your story as a testament of His glory; to set the captives free.

You were created to conquer and overcome every obstacle of your life. You were designed to possess the land that rightfully belongs to you. The Lord gave us dominion and power over the earth and has given us all power over the enemy (**Genesis 1:26-28** and **Luke 10:19**). He made us the head and not the tail; above and not beneath (**Deuteronomy 28:13**). The Lord is so gracious to us in that not only has He given us the right to reign and rule, but He has given us a continuous supply of help with the power of the Holy Ghost. The Holy Ghost is the Lord's Spirit, and He was gifted to us to lead, comfort, advise, teach, and give us power. The power of the Holy Ghost enables us with the willpower and strength to carry out and fulfill God's purpose in our lives (**John 14:16, Acts 1:8**, and **Philippians 2:13**). When I decided that I no longer wanted to be stressed about my finances and not having enough to survive, I had to call on my best friend and my helper, the Holy Ghost. I needed the strength, knowledge, and understanding to make the decision to go where no one else in my family has gone. I decided to trust God beyond what I could see in the natural realm, and I allowed him to put His "super" on my "natural." I experienced the *"supernatural"* move of God because of the sacrifice of obedience to His will and not my own.

NOTHING TO LOSE

The Holy Spirit is strategic, and He speaks to you in a way that ignites a fire inside you to level up. One day, I heard him tell me, *"YOU'VE GOT NOTHING TO LOSE, AND YOU HAVE EVERYTHING TO GAIN."* It may seem like you will lose everything if you choose to follow Jesus—but in all actuality, you gain all of His kingdom and its benefits. My problem, like many of us, was that I was so afraid of losing the invisible battle that I could not see that the battle was already won! Jesus has already redeemed us by paying the price of bondage with His blood. He is the bridge that connects us to the Father…and what our Father owns, we own. All you need is *an ear to hear* what the Lord has to say and be *willing* to follow His lead. Your willingness opens the gates of heaven and sets you up so you can live your best life.

I am reminded of the story of Abraham and Isaac. The Lord promised Abraham that he would surely become a great and powerful nation (**Genesis 18:18**). He told him to sacrifice Isaac, his only son, whom he loved, as a burnt offering. When Abraham and Isaac made it to the top of the mountain, Abraham put his son on the altar and was about to slay him. The angel of the Lord called his name from heaven and told him not to lay a hand on the boy. Then there was a ram in the thicket that the Lord provided as the provision. This sacrifice was a necessary test that tested Abraham's obedience, and his response showed that he truly feared and revered God by giving Him his all, even his precious gift that God promised him, which was his son (**Genesis 22:1-12**).

START LIVING AGAIN

The answer to seeing breakthrough in your life is in your sacrifice. Are you willing to give your fears, tears, pains, failures, and dysfunctions to the Lord and let Him make you whole again? All God needs is a YES, and *He'll do the rest*! You don't have to figure it all out, because He's waiting on the other side with His arms open to receive you. The Lord is saying to you today that it is time for you to stop living in fear and start living again. You have been in survival mode, playing it safe, and only trusting in what you can see. But now it is time to get out of survival and into revival! There's so much greatness on the inside of you, and it's time to shine.

Let the light of the Lord that's in you be the light of the world. You are the Glow Up. There are people waiting on your freedom so that they can be free. I want to encourage you to allow the Holy Spirit to download you with a new and creative mindset. You have the power to shape your own world, your future, and your destiny. And if you get a glimpse of what God wants out of your life, write the vision, make it a plan, and run with it (**Habakkuk 2:2**). Because without His vision, you will perish (**Proverbs 28:19**). The Lord is calling you to see with His eyes and identify that your setbacks have set the stage for HIS SETUP!

QUESTIONS FOR REFLECTION

- *What is your "measure of success?" How has it changed over the years as you have matured?*

- *Have you ever "forged a new path," walking a completely different path than the one that you envisioned or trained for? What did that look like? If you have not done so, would you consider it? What would you do if you knew that you could not fail?*

CHAPTER 13

DESTINED FOR GREATNESS: STEPS TO LIVING THE ABUNDANT LIFE

Breaking free from the ***fear*** *of poverty* is no easy task! It requires sacrifice, obedience, commitment, humility, focus, and faith. It also requires you to completely change your mindset to a whole new set of standards. The old way of thinking is not going to produce new results nor will it allow you to live an abundant life. You have to kill your flesh DAILY, constantly rejecting the things you desire in exchange for the things that God desires. When you kill the flesh, you change the game that the enemy wants you to play! He wants to use your mind as his playground and the spirit of fear as his merry-go-round. He wants you to continue making choices and behaving in such a way that you stay stuck in cycles of poverty. *He wants you to never question your power or your authority that has been given to us by Christ Jesus!* All he wants for you is to remain uneducated about his devices and to never see the glorious light of freedom! Jesus is the freedom I am talking about and without Him, you will never be changed.

The WORD of GOD tell us to *"Delight thyself also in the Lord: and he shall give thee the desires of thine heart. Commit thy way unto the Lord; trust also in him; and he shall bring it to pass"* (**Psalm 37:4-5**). We cannot do anything without the Lord's help, and we certainly cannot *change our mindset* without first knowing His mindset! The Lord has given us the mind of Christ (**Philippians 2:5**), therefore, we have access to the abundant life that Jesus promised (**John 10:10**). The word "delight" according to Strong's Concordance means *"to be delicate, to be happy about, and to make sport of."* And the word "commit" means *"to remove, roll away, seek occasion, trust."* This ultimately means make it a habit of constantly seeking God's will for your life, trusting in His promises (His Word), and committing to the process. We can be assured that once we commit and hand over our plans and our will to the Lord, then we will see major *breakthroughs* in our personal lives, our family, our emotions, our relationships, our careers, and our finances!

Breakthrough is a sign of abundant living! When I think of breakthrough, I think of a tall brick wall preventing me from getting to the other side. It is so tall that when I look up, it seems as if it is thousands of feet in the air. There is no way around it because it is as wide as it as tall. I see myself with a hammer, a chisel, or some sort of tool in my hand, where I am constantly hitting or chipping away at its layers, piece by piece, day by day, and night by night. However, there is no sign of progression! Then, when I am exhausted, tired, and ready to give up, I see a small hole where light is peering through! In this small hole, I can see signs of life because I see light, and I can also hear movement on the other side. So, I start to work harder and move faster, causing more layers to chip away. And only after a few more seconds, I hear a loud *BOOM*, and the entire brick wall falls to the ground. I can finally see the other side, and it is the most beautiful thing that I have ever seen. Every stressor, every hurt, every pain, every negative thought, every amount of fear that I once had is now completely erased. My mind is opened, my hearing is sharp, I can see all of my prayers being answered, and I fill a burden lifted off of me. I feel free, I feel at peace, and I feel safe. I am leaping with joy and gladness, thanking the Lord that I am finally free and able to tangibly grab hold of the promises that He promised me! This is what breakthrough looks like.

Another example of breakthrough can be applied to our physical well-being. Have you ever had a fever? Have you ever had chills? When a person is ill, they may experience periods of cold then hot, and hot then cold. What's going on is warfare within the body. The body is fighting a foreign invader, and the physical symptoms are the manifestation of that battle. During the times of fever and chills, one may feel worse before they get better, because the intensity of the warfare has peaked. We all know, or should know, that in a battle, there is always a climax—a point where something has got to give. After the worst of the worst, the battle is won when the fever breaks! At this point, you stop having fever and chills, and you are no longer ill. This means that the body has won the war and rid the body of the foreign invader. Now, your health is completely restored. The fever breaking is symbolic of breakthrough in our lives; and once you are set free from the things that are preventing you from thriving and living, then you are able to reach a breakthrough.

Breakthrough is a weapon for abundant living! Abundant living is the promise that every believer in Jesus Christ has access to! The word "abundance" according to Merriam Webster means, *"an ample quantity, affluence, wealth, a relative degree of plentifulness."* After you have broken down all the walls: old traditions, old systems, and old mindsets, then you can live a faith-filled and fearless life. To have an abundance of something means that you have everything you need to be successful, joyful, and influential. You lack nothing and have no need for anything less than what your daddy God gives you. When the world is in complete chaos, and it seems as though everything in your own world is falling apart, you can rest in knowing that *the Lord is the Prince of Peace, and he gives you the peace that surpasses all understanding!* He does this because *you have trusted and kept your eyes on HIM* (**Isaiah 9:6**, **Philippians 4:7**, and **Isaiah 26:3**). When you put your trust in the Lord, you make a decision to never go back to a world full of fear, darkness, and confusion. This is freedom and abundant living!

Abundant living requires a P.E.A.C.E. OF MIND! The Holy Spirit downloaded this acronym to me to give you practical ways of living and the next steps to *remaining free*. In order to break free from the fear of poverty and live the abundant life, **you must…**

- *Position Yourself*

- *Examine Your Life and Circumstances*

- *Adjust Your Attitude*

- *Commit to the Process*

- *Encourage Yourself*

Below is a brief explanation of each and practical ways to know what freedom is, what freedom looks like, and how to walk it out!

P-POSITION YOURSELF

It is important that you get yourself into a state of vulnerability with the Lord. You have to be open to the idea that the Lord does not want to **condemn you** *for* your past, He wants to **heal you** *from* your past! *"There is therefore now no condemnation to them who are in Christ Jesus who walk not after the flesh, but after the spirit"* (**Romans 8:1**). Did you know that Jesus heals our broken hearts and binds all of our wounds (**Psalm 147:3**)? He's the *best* doctor…the *ultimate* healer…and He is *calling you* to His operating room. He wants to conduct surgery and give you a brand-new heart, one that's healthy and strong! A heart that is receptive to HIS LOVE! He loves you so much that He gave His only begotten son, Jesus, to take all of your cares, fears, anxieties, illnesses, diseases, and issues, and nail them to the cross (**John 3:16** and **Colossians 2:14**). There is an open invitation to allow Him into your heart. Once you accept the invitation, then you will see restoration and revival. You will see breakthrough and freedom, and you will live an overflow of love, resources, and provision.

When you position yourself, you are basically saying that you are tired of doing things your way that produce no results, and you are accepting Jesus as the Master who has the Master Plan. In my journey with the Lord,

I simply asked the Lord to help me come out of poverty. I knew that I was born into it; but as I learned more about Him, I realized that this was not God's plan for my life. I asked God to give me wisdom in making decisions that would ultimately impact my future, my emotions, my relationships, my careers, my finances, etc. Seeking the face of the Lord and His wisdom is the key to positioning yourself. It opens you up to His protection, provision, and purpose. **Matthew 6:33** explains it this way: *"Seek ye first the kingdom of God and his righteousness and all these things shall be added unto you."* When you look for God in all situations and you study the Scriptures in the Bible, your relationship with HIM strengthens and develops into a healthy two-way communication system. He can now download all the blueprints to overcoming barriers in your life and provides you with the step-by-step process to freedom.

With this being said, you will have to sacrifice your own desires and be obedient to what the Lord tells you to do! For example, when I decided to come out of debt, the Lord showed me that I must write down all of my debts, then look at income and my spending habits. He highlighted where my money was being spent and how the items I purchased were not necessities. He showed me that I spent a lot of money on food alone, particularly restaurants, and that I needed to let that go. I sacrificed the pleasure of eating out with family and friends in order to save and use that money to pay off debt. The good thing about it was not only was I able to save money, but I was also saving inches off my waistline! Another example is that I looked at my cable bill and decided that TV was not a necessity, it was a privilege. With all the technology in the world, the Firestick, the Roku, the internet etc., I could easily view TV shows, movies, or the news for little to no cost. I am not a big TV person to begin with, but the Lord showed me that instead of paying an additional $40 a month for TV that I barely watch, I could use that money to pay off a credit card! In addition, the Lord asked me to stop shopping (for clothes, jewelry, etc.) in order to save money. Shopping was a huge sacrifice for me since I absolutely love shopping. I am that person that can spend hours in the mall and never get tired. I knew that if I wanted to be financially free, that I would have to give up on this area of spending in order to save in another area.

Now, for some people, resisting going to restaurants, cutting off the TV, or not shopping is a bit extreme, but sacrifice requires extreme decision making. You have to completely cut the relationship ties and idolization of materialistic things in order to put the Lord back into His rightful place; in the front seat of your heart! When you allow the Lord to take first place and priority in your heart, He will show you what's on His heart. A good way to find this out is to simply ask God, *"Lord, what's on **your** heart today?"* You will soon start to feel a conviction about how you are doing things. It is basically a heart check. Conviction causes you to come to your senses, to see things as God sees them, and to desire to *do better* and to *be better*. The glory or the benefit of all of the sacrifice and obedience is that God has something bigger and better for us on the other side. Financial stewardship and financial freedom allow you to manage your finances and resources well.

E-EXAMINE YOUR LIFE AND YOUR CIRCUMSTANCES

Everyone should examine their own life and the circumstances that shape their decision making. You have to realize that you are human, and that you are not perfect. God doesn't want you to be perfect—He wants you to realize that you can do nothing on your own, but it is HIS SPRIT that will guide you in all Truth **(John 16:13)**. When I looked at everything in my life, it was a mess. The mother and father wounds, emotional instability, unhealthy relationships, career ups and downs…it was all a hot mess! I had to come to the reality that everything was out of control and that I needed order. I needed a way to make sense of what was going on, and I needed to know if this was the way my life was going to be forever. I had to be true to myself and true to God. I looked at some of my circumstances and was sick to my stomach, unsure of how things started or how to get out of them.

Examining your life requires you digging into your past and identifying entry points where the devil came in and caused confusion, trauma, pain, and a misrepresentation of the Father. It is extremely important that you ask God to show you where the entry points are in your life and how to close those doors. Most of us avoid going into our past because it is too ugly, it is painful, and we feel ashamed, condemned and worthless. We don't want to address any issues because it requires that *we do something about it, which is work.*

> Once you acknowledge something, it makes you accountable, so most of us would rather sweep it under the rug, and keep it moving.

This was the case for me when it came to my personal family relationships. The emotional hurt and pain that I experienced with my mother and father wounds was an area that cut so deeply that I created a vow to never let anyone *"fully in."* I suppressed all of my emotions and brushed them off as if I was okay. I eventually convinced myself that I *was* okay and that I would never need anyone for anything. My "low-level thinking" created a hindrance to my healing and deliverance because I was unwilling to allow the pain to surface and deal with the real issues.

One day, while speaking to the Father, He allowed me to think about the circumstances that surrounded my pain. He showed me that my mother and father only did what they were taught, and that I could no longer hold them accountable. *The Lord taught me to love them as He loves them!* The way I did this was the leading of His Spirit. The Holy Spirit had me to pray this prayer: *"Lord, let me see them the way you see them."* This type of prayer is dangerous, yet it is a safe place! It is safe because you remove yourself from the equation, and you see others in a new light. You see people and situations as a spiritual battle, not a personal one. Therefore, you release yourself from frustration, anger, bitterness, and unforgiveness, and you protect yourself from illness, sickness, and disease. It gives you the power and authority to destroy every plan, plot, and scheme that the devil has set out before you and to reconcile healthy relationships with your family. If we can be real with ourselves and allow compassion to flood our hearts, then you will see people as human beings who are capable of making mistakes just as we are.

Our lives and our circumstances allow us *to see where we are, to see where we are going, and to see where we need to be!*

A-ADJUST YOUR ATTITUDE

There are many walls in our lives that represent old systems and traditions. We have built our own mental prisons and have given the enemy the keys to the entrance by our way of thinking and what we say out of our own mouths. The Bible clearly states that *"as a man thinketh in his heart, so is he…"* and *"death and life are in the power of the tongue: and they that love it shall eat the fruit thereof"* (**Proverbs 27:3** and **Proverbs 18:21**). What you think in your heart and what you say out of your mouth has the power to shape your circumstances. When the Lord created the heavens and earth, it was without form…until he SPOKE out of HIS MOUTH. He framed *the world* with *HIS WORD* (**Genesis 1:1-3** and **Hebrews 11:4**)! You have to make a decision to change the way you think, speak, feel, and behave. Once you decide to come out of agreement with "low-level thinking," then you will see your true purpose and you will excel in every area of your life.

I had a wake-up call, and that wake-up call was the reality that I would be stuck in a world that did not bring me joy, peace, or satisfaction. I lived in a reality that poverty was the norm and that I was destined for this type of lifestyle because it was all that I saw within my family. Many people won't admit this, but they have been too lazy to do what it takes to see change in their lives. They are not willing to sacrifice their own selfish desires for a better life because it is too uncomfortable. Don't you know that God will allow circumstances to happen to get you out of your comfort zone? He will apply pressure when needed if you are resistant. He is not doing this to make you do something for Him, He is doing it to show you His plans of freedom for your life!

During the season of my life where I experienced back-to-back layoffs as a nurse practitioner, I didn't know that God was trying to wake me up to show me more about myself and my future. Although, I questioned, *"Why is this happening?"* I didn't sit long enough to hear what He had to say concerning my situation. I was too wrapped up in my own self, struggling, living in fear, fighting my own battles, and learning to survive the only way I knew how. These layoffs were distractions to prevent me from the real issue at hand and that was to keep me in a generation cycle of poverty and to keep me from that promise that the Lord is my provision and that He has called me to be a generator of wealth! Wealth is more than just money. It is a resource of knowledge, wisdom, creativity, resources, strategy, etc.

See, we live in a microwave society, where we want the quick route, the quick answers, and the quick results, but we don't want to put in the work! The hardest part is actually not doing the work, it is *making up in your mind* that you will do whatever it takes to get to the finish line! I always ask myself and my friends, *"How badly do you want it?"* Some of my friends look at me like I'm crazy when I ask this, but this question truly address the posture of your heart. What I mean is that if you want to be free from something badly enough, then you will be willing to go to extreme measures and do whatever it takes to overcome it. For example, when I decided that debt would *not* be my portion and I wanted to get out, I made up in my mind that if I had to live paycheck to paycheck while aggressively destroying debt, then that's what I was going to do. I had to sacrifice having some "extra cash" in my pocket and stop the pleasurable shopping for my future! It was a daily battle in my mind, and I had to renew my mind daily, looking at the bigger picture. Not only was I going to be debt-free, but I was building my legacy and setting up a future for my children and for generations to come. I was also creating a doorway for myself to save, to invest in property, and to buy the things I wanted.

If you are in a place in your life where you are tired of the "same ol', same ol'," and you are ready to GET OUT of your mind, then consider this a great place to start. Adjusting your attitude or the way you think allows you to think more positively about yourself. You will start taking yourself more seriously and seeing yourself as worthy. You must renew your mind daily! It is an essential principle to put into practice daily. **Romans 12:2** states, *"And be not conformed to this world: but be ye transformed by the renewing of your mind, they ye may prove what is that good, and acceptable, and perfect, will of God."* Renewing your mind requires a constant tearing down of thoughts and behaviors that have once produced unfruitful results in your life (**2 Corinthians 10:5**). You don't think the same way as you once did because you see that you are closer to freedom more now than ever. And when old thoughts or patterns try to creep back in, you have to remind yourself that that is no longer the life you want to live.

There will be times in your life where you will have to go against the grain and do what's best for you. Some people may not understand the choices you make; but as long as you are not conforming to the ways of this world (how everyone else thinks) and you are seeking the Lord, then you are *in the will of God.* Remember that *change is good, change is necessary, and change will change your life!*

C-COMMIT TO THE PROCESS

Once you break through the challenges of dealing with your past, posturing your heart, examining your life, and changing the way you think, then you are ready to put in the work! You must commit to the process and practice your new way of living. What I love about "true" commitment is that you can fall off and still get back on the bandwagon. The Lord isn't interested in seeing how many times you fall, but He *is* interested in your commitment. Will you continue to seek His face for continual guidance, especially when you've tried one way, and it didn't work out well? This is what commitment looks like. Remember, we are not perfect. We may stumble or fall sometimes, but the Lord is always there to pick us up **(Proverbs 24:16)**. The Father will not leave you to be a failure. He honors every attempt to carry out His will!

Deciding to commit is a step of courage and faith. You must put your faith in God knowing that He will carry you through your process and give you courage to keep moving forward. The devil will try to shoot his fiery darts of distractions and sow seeds of discouragement, but God will remind you that *"you are more than a conqueror through Jesus Christ who loves you"* **(Romans 8:37)**. The way you move forward is by staying the course. Start your day with talking to the Lord and asking Him to prepare you for each day. He will start downloading His plan and creative ways of how to conquer your time. You **must not** lose focus. You have to set goals for yourself, make them measurable, and keep the bigger picture at the forefront. In addition, make a schedule, and stick to it. Create a "To-Do" list with the most important tasks listed first. This will help you stay organized.

When I committed the process of being free of poverty, I would write my goals down. From a financial standpoint, I would write out my goals and plans to pay off debt. I put every credit card in a box and listed out the months in which I was going to pay them off. I then took the total amount of debt and divided it by the number of months that I was going to pay it off. Furthermore, I looked at my income and expenses or other bills and decided if I paid a certain amount every two weeks (per paycheck), would I have enough to pay my other essential bills (lights, gas, mortgage, food, etc.). If I could pay a certain amount and have all of my essentials covered then it was a good plan. However, if it would leave me struggling, then I had to change the plan. The overall goal was to meet my essential needs but to also pay high amounts of debt in a short period of time. I would often revisit my plans to see if I was meeting my goals. There would be times where I would have to readjust the amount of payment due to extra unforeseen finances such as a doctor's bill or added expenses on my HOA fees.

Every time I paid a bill or debt off and saw the high amount going towards that bill, my flesh would say, *"Wow, that's a lot of money. Do you know what you could do with that amount?"* I had to kill my flesh and remind myself that the more I pay off, the sooner I will be out of debt and be set free. I was committed to the process because I was looking forward to the benefit of my changed behavior. Therefore, I did not question or doubt the process that I needed to go through. I was consistent in revising my plan as needed and addressing the issues that were hindering my progress. When you are in your process of commitment, you have to remind yourself daily that it is all worth it in the end! You will come out on top and defeat the enemy once and for all. Abundant living is not for the weak—it is for the ones who are consistent in the process.

E-ENCOURAGE YOURSELF

The more fearful you are, the more fear becomes empowered! Fear is a major weapon that the enemy uses to paralyze us in our walk with God, and it prevents us from walking into the door of abundance. The power of fear has caused many of us to stop living life, period. Many of us stopped progressing in life because we get discouraged! Discouragement leads to stagnation. We cannot keep allowing frustrations and setbacks to block our motivation to keep moving forward. **We must use discouragement as our encouragement!** When you are encouraged, you have *the courage* to do things you have never done before, *the faith* to move mountains, and *the power* to destroy every demonic force in your life. Encouragement is the powerful weapon that God staffs His people with to reinforce His sovereignty and our victory. It is the antidote to abundant living!

Encouragement is God's way of cheering us on and inspiring us to live better lives. He inspires us to be the BEST VERSION of ourselves! His inspiration is found in His Word, and it equips us with confidence, hope, and instruction. The Word of God tells us that *"All Scripture is given by inspiration of God and is profitable for doctrine, for reproof, for correction, for instructions in righteousness"* **(2 Timothy 3:16)**. The Scriptures reveal the true nature of God and inspire us to live a life where we can learn His Truth, be corrected when we are in the wrong, and give us the blueprints to live righteously according to His righteousness. A good way to measure your life and determine if you are doing what God has called you to do is to measure it up with His Word. This means that you need to find a Scripture or two and apply it to every area of your life (health, finances, relationships, and careers). For example, if I am having a hard time dealing with a difficult boss who is mean and treats me unfairly for no reason, then I have to find out how the Lord will handle the situation. The one Scripture that comes to mind is in **Matthew 5:44** which states, *"But I say unto you, 'Love your enemies, bless them that curse you, do good to them that hate you, and pray for them which despitefully use you, and persecute you.'"* This Scripture is telling me that I need to pray for that boss and bless them regardless of how they are treating me. My flesh may want to curse them, and I might even start to hate them, but this is not the character of God. His Word checks our heart posture and causes us to love even when it is difficult to love.

The Lord uses His Word to encourage, and He also uses people to carry out His Word, especially in rough times. Have you ever been in a difficult situation where you didn't see a way out but one of your friends gave you the perfect solution? Have you ever had a bad day and received a text message that said, *"I love you"* or *"I appreciate you?"* Have you ever felt insecure about yourself, and someone told you that you were beautiful and worthy? Or felt rejected and abandoned and someone told you, *"I got you. I am here for you!"* I have been in all of these situations, and I can honestly say that the responses changed my perspective of life and lifted my spirits. It gave me a boost in my confidence, and it solidified my faith in God. It taught me that our God is a good, good Father, and He uses encouraging words, through people, to show His love, and His dedications to seeing us win!

Lastly, we have to fully engage ourselves in the Word of God to encourage ourselves. Our example is shown in the Bible where King David literally had to encourage himself during a distressful time in his life. **1 Samuel 30:6** states, *"And David was greatly distressed; for the people spake of stoning him, because the soul of all the people was grieved, every man for his sons and for his daughters: but David encouraged himself in the LORD his God."* There will be times in your life where you will be in the heat of the battle, and there is no one to call. You may not have anyone cheering you on all the time, so you must find safety in the Word of God, to help you get through the rough periods of your time. I love the Word of God because the more you learn and study the Scriptures, the more you build your faith. *"So then faith comes by hearing and hearing by the word of God"* (**Romans 10:17**).

Building your faith is like the relationship you have with your bank account. You can either make a deposit or a withdrawal. In your spiritual faith bank, you must deposit the Scriptures you have learned, and write them on your heart. Then, when you are in a moment of fear, distress, or discouragement, you can make a withdrawal by praying those Scriptures. Those Scriptures will bring complete peace to your mind and to your life, but once the battle is over, you must continue to add and replace the Scriptures that you withdrew. Otherwise, you will run out of your strength and your source of life. Just like with a regular bank account, you cannot just make withdrawals and have no deposits; otherwise, your funds will be depleted and you will end up bankrupt. It is like dealing with the cycle of poverty, living paycheck to paycheck; but instead of living, you are dying, day by day. Don't let your faith bank run dry as it is the source of your life!

The Lord wants to move you out of a place of hopelessness and into a place of expectancy! He wants you to expect the best out of your life and to execute with great power and authority. The power and authority that we have is our faith in Jesus Christ who promised us *THE ABUNDANT LIFE*. Faith removes fear! The more faith you have, the more you become empowered because fear isn't an option. And when you are empowered, you encourage others to be empowered! Hence, you become a fearless generation! The devil has been working overtime to kill, to steal, and to destroy your purpose and your destiny, BUT GOD has established His covenant with you, from the beginning of time, and there is an expected end for your life (**John 10:10** and **Jeremiah 29:11**). God will do whatever it takes to complete the good work in you that He started (**Philippians 1:6**). It is your time to shine…but be in expectancy! *Expect to overcome fear! Expect to destroy poverty! Expect a mindset change! Expect to level up! Expect to come out on top! Expect to change the world! And most importantly, expect to "Live the Abundant Life"!*

PRAISE FOR
"BREAKING FREE
FROM THE FEAR OF POVERTY"

I met Stefani Alexander at All Nations Worship Assembly Chicago in March of 2019. I was the lead teacher of a Foundations class at ANWA University, and she was serving as a first time "shadowing" teacher. She was a great help to me, and the students spoke highly of her. Her kindness, enthusiasm, and willingness to become part of the team was a big hit. We instantly became a co-teaching team!

Stefani loves people, and it shows in whatever she does. She is always willing to help wherever needed. Excellence, beauty, love, compassion, and creativity are gifts she displays freely; and her creativity comes alive when she is assigned or thinks of a new project. In the midst of all of the gifts, projects, and her ministry call, she is focused and well-organized. We can be in a conversation about a project; and before we're done brainstorming, she already has a framework in place for what we need to do!

I am much older than Stefani, and I am always reminding her of what a blessing she is to me. I consider our relationship as one of mother and daughter, close friends, and mentorship. **Proverbs 27:17** says, *"As iron sharpens iron, so a man sharpens the countenance of his friend."*

I believe what Stefani has written in this book was ordained by God and will certainly bless the life of every reader. I know it will display love, kindness, creativity, and the compassion that flows from her heart. Read this book and increase!

~ Minister Linda Cobb
Beauty for Ashes Ministries,
Gary, IN

I met Stefani in July 2011 through our sorority, Elogeme Adolphi Christian Sorority, Inc. Stefani asked me for a ride to our annual Summit Conference, and we have been the best of friends ever since. I have known her now for eight years. She is full of wisdom, and I can always call on her when I need advice. She has a passion for people, and she always likes to see them on top, no matter what they are going through. I have learned a lot from Stefani. She has taught me how to properly handle life's problems and how to transition through difficult stages of life.

Stefani mentored me through nursing school where I learned how to develop an eye for detail, which helped to shape me into being the nurse that I am today. She is a great mentor, listener, and motivator. She is my "Hype-Woman." She is reliable and a woman of her word! Our friendship is full of laughter, fun, and honesty. She knows how to bring the best out in her friends. I love her to life. She is doing great things, and I know that this book will bless everyone who reads it!

~ **ASHLEY KING, RN**
Elogeme Adolphi Christian Sorority, Inc.,
Peoria, IL

It's not often you meet a person like Stefani! She literally has a heart for people; and as she opens her heart, out pours compassion, love, giving, and sharing. Stefani will give of herself until it hurts. Her focus is to teach and evangelize the Word of God at any cost. When I think of Stefani, I think of a sharpshooter in the spirit realm! God gives her a person to mentor and cultivate, and her focus is for them to experience heaven on earth. Stefani spreads the joy of the Lord wherever she goes and has a smile for everyone she encounters. When Stefani enters a room, the whole atmosphere shifts; she's a beacon of light to me and to my family!

Stefani is saved, sanctified, filled with the Holy Ghost, Fire Baptized, the salt of the earth, and is always ready to answer why she believes. She is always willing to lay aside her own agenda for the Kingdom of God to help someone else, so that's why I'm proud to call her my spiritual daughter and more importantly, the daughter of the Most High God!

Stefani exemplifies a follower of Christ, and her aim is to walk and execute the goodness of God in the land of the living!

~ **Bernadine Harris**
Temple Building Ministries,
Crown Point, IN

Growing up with Stefani, our house was always full of laughter and jokes with her at center stage. She could always make light of the hardships we faced being raised by a single mother, who occasionally worked two jobs to financially sustain our family. I remember a time when Stefani and I were grounded in our shared bedroom. Instead of joining me down a pity road, she decided that we should play a game instead which instantly filled the room with joy. I can't remember what we did to get sent to our room. I also can't remember the game we played. But I will never forget the warm, comforting feeling that entered our room as we shared in a moment of pure, innocent laughter from whatever quest Stefani was taking us on that day. Today, she remains that same beam of joy in my life as well as the lives of many others.

Stefani has always been the type of sister worth mimicking. Apart from her lighthearted character, she has never joked about spiritual warfare, especially poverty. For as long as I can remember, Stefani has declared wealth over her life even when her natural circumstances have suggested otherwise. I have observed her gracefully walk out many trials in her life while maintaining a pure heart aimed toward setting others free from physical and spiritual bondages. As a first-generation college graduate, Stefani set the standard in our family by proving that an abundant life was truly obtainable. While it has always been a joy to celebrate her accomplishments, I'm even more proud of how she responds to trauma.

I have witnessed Stefani experience what has looked like back-to-back setbacks. From multiple job layoffs to recovering after a critical car accident, her life within itself provides a template to others on what it means to trust God to carry you through. Her consistent faith walk is a powerful evangelistic weapon that reaches to the hardest of hearts, declaring that with God, all things are possible. As you read Stefani's book, you will surely become inspired to step into the full, abundant life that God has promised you!

~ **SHARON ALEXANDER-JENKINS**
Evangelist, Entrepreneur,
Chicago, IL

ABOUT THE AUTHOR

Stefani Alexander is a dynamic evangelist, teacher of the Word of God, motivational speaker, author, and a board-certified women's healthcare nurse practitioner (WHNP-BC) by trade. She encompasses the fire of God, setting souls on fire for the Lord. Her heart's desire is that every individual escape the snare of hell and be delivered into the soul-satisfying thirst for our Lord and Savior Jesus Christ. Her fire has ignited others to remain strong in their faith for God and has given them the courage to live their best life. She brings HOPE to the hopeless and LOVE to the broken!

Stefani started her ministry as a young child, preaching and teaching the kids on the block in her backyard. As she grew older, the Lord illuminated her calling as an evangelist, and she has always been on fire for saving lost souls for Christ. Throughout her lifelong journey of serving God, she has experienced many adversities tied to the spirit of poverty. From 2012 to 2019, she experienced four layoffs from five different jobs as a WHNP. This devastation caused hesitancy, anxiety, and fear in all areas of her life, particularly financial security. However, the Lord raised Stefani to be a mighty deliverer for this generation in order to demonstrate the power of God that one can be *born* into poverty, but not *live* in poverty!

Throughout this book, Stefani will to take you on a journey of how she was born into poverty, and how she no longer lives in poverty. Passionate about getting out of debt, tired of being laid off, and with her obedience to the Lord, she decided to take the steps needed to be free, despite every life experience, every relationship, and every setback that was set up to break her down and destroy God's purpose in her life, she broke free from poverty so that *you* could be free!

RESOURCES

If you would like to begin pursuing a debt-free life, here are some resources that I highly recommend:

Financial Peace University by Dave Ramsey
 Website: www.daveramsey.com

His and Her Money by Talaat and Tai McNeely
 Website: www.hisandhermoney.com

CONTACT THE AUTHOR

If you would like to contact Stefani, you may do so at

stefani.alexander1@gmail.com

CPSIA information can be obtained
at www.ICGtesting.com
Printed in the USA
BVHW040643120121
597555BV00013B/106